Polity Histories series

Jeff Kingston, *Japan*
David W. Lesch, *Syria*
Dmitri Trenin, *Russia*

China

Kerry Brown

polity

First published in 2020 by Polity Press

Polity Press
65 Bridge Street
Cambridge CB2 1UR, UK

Polity Press
101 Station Landing
Suite 300
Medford, MA 02155, USA

ISBN-13: 978-1-5095-4147-8
ISBN-13: 978-1-5095-4148-5 (pb)

A catalogue record for this book is available from the British Library.

Library of Congress Cataloging-in-Publication Data
Names: Brown, Kerry, 1967- author.
Title: China / Kerry Brown.
Description: Medford, MA : Polity, 2020. | Series: Polity histories |
    Summary: "A sharp and smart history of 20th and 21st century China"--
    Provided by publisher.
Identifiers: LCCN 2020000126 (print) | LCCN 2020000127 (ebook) | ISBN
    9781509541478 (hardback) | ISBN 9781509541485 (paperback) | ISBN
    9781509541492 (epub)
Subjects: LCSH: China--History--1949-1976. | China--History--1976-2002. |
    China--History--2002-
Classification: LCC DS777.55 .B697 2020 (print) | LCC DS777.55 (ebook) |
    DDC 951.05--dc23
LC record available at https://lccn.loc.gov/2020000126
LC ebook record available at https://lccn.loc.gov/2020000127

Typeset in 11 on 13 Berkeley by Servis Filmsetting Ltd, Stockport, Cheshire
Printed and bound in Great Britain by CPI Group (UK) Ltd, Croydon

For further information on Polity, visit our website: politybooks.com

Contents

Abbreviations

BRI   Belt and Road Initiative
CCDI   Central Commission for Discipline and Inspection
CPC   Communist Party of China
CR   Cultural Revolution
GATT   General Agreement on Tariffs and Trade
PLA   People's Liberation Army
PRC   People's Republic of China
SEZ   Special Economic Zone
TVEs   Town and Village Enterprises
WTO   World Trade Organization

Dedicated to the memory of Christopher Henson,
and to his wife, Sally.

Acknowledgements

I would like to thank Louise Knight at Polity Press for commissioning this work, and her colleagues, including copy-editor Justin Dyer, for their assistance. I am also grateful for the help of Yi Wushuang, Huang Yiqin, and Xuan Li for reading early drafts and making comments. Remaining errors remain solely mine.

About the Author

Kerry Brown is Professor of Chinese Studies and Director of the Lau China Institute, King's College, London, and Associate Fellow on the Asia Pacific Programme at Chatham House, London. From 2012 to 2015, he was Professor of Chinese Politics and Director of the China Studies Centre at the University of Sydney. Prior to this, from 1998 to 2005, he served as a diplomat in the British Foreign and Commonwealth Office, and then from 2006 to 2012 was Senior Fellow and then Head of the Asia Programme at Chatham House. He was Director of the Europe China Research and Advice Network (ECRAN) funded by the European Union from 2011 to 2014. He is the author of twenty books, the most recent of which are *China's Dream: The Culture of Chinese Communism and the Secret Sources of its Power* (Cambridge: Polity, 2018) and *The Trouble with Taiwan: History, the United States and a Rising China* (London: Zed Books, 2019).

1

China's Arduous March to Modernity

Chinese history is long and complex. It is a story that splits into many different themes and plots. Trying to understand China without having at least some knowledge of this historical background is, nevertheless, impossible. This is particularly true today, when current Chinese leaders daily appeal to the glorious, unique past of their country as a source of their authority and power in the present. The complexity of this history, however, means that there are many different interpretations and meanings that can be harvested from it. This book aims to present at least some of these, and show why they are important.

Despite China's global prominence in the twenty-first century, these Chinese histories are not well known by people in Europe or the United States (broadly what we can call 'the West'). This lack of knowledge is compounded by the politicized way that China's history is told within the current People's Republic of China (PRC). This book aims at helping to rectify this situation, giving those with no specialist engagement with China a workable outline by which to make sense of this vast story.

One aim of this book is to demonstrate that, however marginal China may have seemed in much of the period since the mid-nineteenth century, for a country and a culture accounting for a fifth of humanity, its story is a global one. It was an aberration that so little of this story was known outside of China. What we are witnessing now is a long-overdue correction to this imbalance – something that should have been done earlier.

What is China?

Before grappling with Chinese history, we have to ask a more fundamental question: what is China? Shanghai-based contemporary academic Ge Zhaoguang acknowledges that the answer to this question is intimately linked to historical issues. Speaking to the debate about whether the current PRC has grown from what has been called a 'civilizational state' based on cultural influence not tied to particular geographical boundaries, or is a real empire exercising hard territorial power, he proposes a number of orientating ideas. The first of these is that 'even though China's borders have often changed, the central region has been relatively stable, becoming very early on a place with a commonly recognized territory and unified politics, nationality, and culture: this region also comprised a historical world.'[1] He also argues that Han (dominant ethnic group) culture, for all its diversity, 'extended across time in this region, forming a clear and distinct cultural identity and cultural mainstreams'. Supplementing this was 'a traditional Chinese world of ideas', and the sense of 'cultural continuity'. This mixture of geography, culture, ethnicity, and belief systems created an organic whole, something that can link the earliest dynasties for the Qin two centuries before the time of Christ, to the Tang from the seventh century, and the Song, Yuan, Ming, and Qing imperial eras that covered the millennium from 960 up to 1911.

The distinctive result of this is that '"China" has had both the characteristics of a traditional imperial state and aspects that resemble early modern nation-states; it has resembled *both* a modern nation-state and a traditional civilizational community.'[2] Despite the efforts of the post-modern deconstructers, for Ge 'China' is a definite thing, and it has cohesiveness, continuity with past entities occupying broadly the same geographical space and ethnic, cultural, and ideological components. It is far more than a geographical idea. Chinese leaders today echo this when they claim that their country, despite being founded in its current guise in 1949, has a continuous civilizational integrity stretching back further than anywhere else. Speaking soon after becoming General Secretary of the Communist Party of China (CPC) in 2012, shortly before becoming President a few months later, Xi Jinping declared that 'the Chinese nation has an unbroken history of more than 5,000 years of civilization. It has created a rich and profound culture and has made an unforgettable contribution to the progress of human civilization.'[3]

Every part of Ge's ideas, and those contained in Xi's

statement, could be contested – and they frequently are. The '5,000-year history' claim makes as much sense as saying Europe, with all its experience of fragmentation and complexity, has a common root going back to ancient Greece 2,500 years ago. For sure, there are unifying threads; but they are just that: threads. For long stretches, the geographical space we call China today was divided. There were multiple states and empires. As for Han ethnic continuity supplying this area of commonality, in the last 1,000 years, previous Chinese states have been under non-Han rule for over a third of this time. The last imperial dynasty, that of the Qing (1644–1912), was, as historians in recent decades have argued, one ruled by the Manchu group, extending far beyond the historical limits of previous Chinas, and connected to Inner Asia and other geographies through geographical annexation. As historian Timothy Brook argues, the modern centralized Chinese state was as much the creation of the Mongolian conquests of the thirteenth century, and their imposition of rigid rule, as something that links back to the Golden Age of the Tang and is derived from the state ideology adopted then of Confucianism and its highly hierarchical notion of order (608–912 CE).[4]

Despite this huge set of issues, one thing is indisputable. 'Chinese history' is seen as an immense source of cultural unity by politicians like Xi. Nor does this just apply to the current Communist leaders. The Nationalist leader Chiang Kai-shek (1887–

1975), head of the Republican government in power up to 1949 before fleeing to Taiwan, spoke in similar ways in the 1930s: 'Through five thousand years of alternate order and confusion and the rise and fall of dynasties, our nation has acquired the virtue of modesty, a sense of honour and the ability to endure insult and shoulder hardships.'[5] Every leader in the People's Republic, from its founder Mao Zedong to Xi, has repeated sentiments similar to these. Each, however, has chosen to accept interpretations which accorded with his own priorities, recognizing how complex and varied a resource 'Chinese history' is.

Mao was the most radical, boldly eschewing much of the heritage of China's historical and political imperial past by castigating it as feudal and exploitative. Despite this, he still asserted a strong sense of pride in aspects of Chinese literature and culture. Mao's posture illustrates the ambiguity of this historical legacy – the ways in which it was a source of suffocating restraint as much as of secure identity. 'Although China is a great nation,' he wrote in 1939, 'and although she is a vast country with an immense population, a long history, a rich revolutionary tradition and splendid historical heritage, her economic, political and cultural development was sluggish for a long time after the transition from a slave to a feudal society.'[6] His successors, Deng Xiaoping (paramount leader from 1978 to the 1990s), Jiang Zemin (President from 1989 to 2003), Hu Jintao (2003 to 2013), and Xi Jinping (President from 2013 to the time of writing), have appealed to 'traditional' Chinese culture as something more positive and unifying than Mao appeared to suggest.

The rehabilitation of the past after Mao's attack has not been easy. The path of modernity since the nineteenth century has involved fierce arguments about what relationship modern leaders need to take to this history, and what sort of resource it offers. The common point is that all eras of modern Chinese history, despite their very different political convictions and attitudes, have been driven by the desire for renewal. Chinese modern history has involved many things: the mission to industrialize, to create national unity, to struggle against colonial interference and achieve national self-determination. But, above all, it has been a history of trying to renew.

China's Struggle to Catch Up

China's engagement with modernity was an arduous one. It has spawned many myths, some of which are unresolved. In recent decades, there has been a lively debate about the issue of why industrialization and economic modernization took the very different trajectories they did in Europe and China. In *The Great Divergence*, historian Kenneth Pomeranz joins those who contest the popular idea that Europe had something unique in terms of its culture and philosophical outlook which meant it was predisposed to innovate and industrialize. 'There is little to suggest,' he writes, 'that western Europe's economy had decisive advantages before [the 1800s], either in its capital stock or economic institutions, that made industrialization highly probable there and unlikely elsewhere.'[7] Rather than attributing Europe's ultimate success in pulling ahead so dramatically in the nineteenth century to holistic explanations that range from the cultural – Max Weber's Protestant work ethic, for instance – to the more overtly economic or political – like the rise of consumption and the prevalence of individualism and its associated governance models – Pomeranz looks at a host of interrelated, but different, more localized causes. Some of these derive from the various forms of resistance to change and transformation within Qing China. Some refer to the strengths of Europe in terms of political and social flexibility. What is indisputable is that in the nineteenth century the Qing was in seemingly irrevocable decline. In gross terms, China ranked as the world's largest single economy up to 1820. But this claim is rendered almost meaningless by the deep structural differences between the Qing's economy and that of, for instance, Great Britain. Nineteenth-century China did not have the same levels of urbanization, infrastructure building, and capital formation that powers like the United States, Great Britain, and Germany did. While its lack of naval assets made it incapable of reaching and impacting on Europe, Europe was more than capable of involving itself directly in China. By 1900, China was weak, exposed, and vulnerable.

These issues are illustrated by one of the key

moments of encounter between the Qing court and an industrialized and modernizing Great Britain approaching its century of radical transformation. The Macartney Mission during the era of George III (r. 1760–1820) is a key moment in the histories of both China and the West. The outcome of this mission was a rejection by the ageing Qianlong emperor (r. 1735–96) of the manufactures and goods offered by the visiting dignitaries. Throughout the whole mission there were many moments of cultural miscommunication. Lord George Macartney's refusal to show his status as a visitor from a vassal state by kowtowing to the emperor and the tortuous negotiations to achieve a way around was one of the most striking. But Macartney's journal recording the visit presents many more examples. On 13 October 1793, he gave vent to his general frustration:

> How are we to reconcile the contradictions that appear in the conduct of the Chinese government towards us? They receive us with the highest distinction, show us every external mark of favour and regard. . . . Yet, in less than a couple of months, they plainly discover that they wish us to be done, refuse our requests without reserve or complaisance, precipitate our departure, and dismiss us dissatisfied; yet no sooner have we taken leave of them than we find ourselves treated with more studied attentions, more marked distinction and less constraint than before. I must endeavour to unravel this mystery if I can.[8]

Macartney's expression of bewilderment has been echoed ever since. In the twenty-first century, the creation of confusion with interlocutors has been one of the consistent characteristics of Chinese negotiating behaviour.

Macartney's mission had limited success. Half a century later, the vast Manchu-run Qing empire was to pit itself against less benign aspects of the West. The first Opium War of 1839 figures in Chinese historiography to this day as inaugurating a period of China as the victim – one it is only now emerging from fully. This involved the British using advanced gunboats to force the Qing to accept the import of opium drugs they had banned because of widespread addiction within the country. Despite this attack, it was domestic challenges that proved more tumultuous in the short term, raising the question of who in the end was most responsible for the country's woeful state: itself or outsiders. The Taiping Rebellion from 1850 to 1864 was the most extreme. Approximately 20 million died from the upheaval caused by the revolt. While it did not finish off the Qing, it contributed to the regime's eventual collapse half a century later. The Taiping remains a bewildering event. Inspired and instigated by Hong Xiuquan (1814–64), a native of Guangdong, it mixed traditional peasant rebellion with a semi-mystical, messianic-style movement. Hong claimed he was the brother of Jesus Christ, setting up a Heavenly Kingdom based in Nanjing. From idealistic beginnings, the rebellion evolved into a civil war. Its destructiveness was compounded by the Second Opium War from 1856 to 1860, one that resulted in the creation of more treaty ports and foreign concessions open to Western powers.

The Key Chinese Modernizers

Many within China acknowledged the critically dangerous position of their country after these crises and the urgent need for modernization to overcome this. Core figures in this modernization effort were Liang Qichao (1873–1929) and Kang Youwei (1858–1927), who supplied key ideas that inspired the 100-day 1898 Minor Reform movement. Their ambitious list of proposals, inspired in part by the example of Japan reforming under the Meiji Restoration, embraced the abolition of the centuries-old examination system, the creation of new universities, the adoption of Western free-market-orientated economic models, and the establishment of a constitutional monarchy. These proposals failed. The sitting emperor Guangxu was placed under a form of house arrest, his powers largely taken from him by the Empress Dowager Ci Xi (1835–1908). Kang and Liang fled to Japan to continue their reformist work. Despite this, these events left a powerful memory, one that remains haunting to this day. 'After the defeat by Japan [in the First Sino-Japanese War of 1894–5],' Liang was to comment many years later, 'people with good minds in the nation really seemed to have met a thunderbolt in a dream. Accordingly, they wondered why the great and grand China should have declined to such a degree, and discovered it was all due to her bad political system.'[9] Within two years, however, the Boxer Rebellion (1899–1901), another hybrid uprising, this time more targeted at foreigners accused of having too much influence in China, resulted in even more punitive indemnities. A decade later, the Qing finally collapsed. China's long imperial history had ended.

The '100 Days' reform's most powerful legacy was the notion of China needing once more to be a wealthy, powerful nation. 'Fuqiang Guojia' was the Chinese expression of this. It gave birth to a sense of nationalism that transcended all social and political boundaries. The founder of the Nationalist Party and, for a brief period, the President of the new Republic, Sun Yat-sen (1866–1925), gave this even sharper definition, along with figures like early Communist movement activist and academic Chen Duxiu (1879–1942). The aim for both was the same: to create a place that was unified, powerful, strong, and no longer victimized. This vision has endured, figuring in the work of Mao Zedong (1894–1976), Chiang Kai-shek, and in writings by intellectuals as disparate as the great author Lu Xun (1881–1936) and the polymath Hu Shih (1881–1962). In this interpretation, China's cultural uniqueness, its extraordinary ancient civilization, was a source not of weakness but of strength. The key task was to modernize and renew it.

Competing Visions: Sun, Chiang, and Mao

In the three decades after the collapse of the Qing, China experienced a period of fragmentation, political instability, and intense aggression from outsiders. Most of this was under the Republican government led, eventually, by Chiang Kai-shek. By the 1930s, the country was called the sick man of Asia. Sun Yat-sen, Chiang Kai-shek, and Mao Zedong offered three competing visions of what needed to be done. Sun had spent less than a hundred days as provisional President of China from January to March 1912, but his influence remains to this day. Writing in 'The Three Principles of the People', he declared in 1922: 'Considering the law of survival of ancient and modern races, if we want to save China and to preserve the Chinese race, we must certainly promote Nationalism.' The key issue was that the Chinese people were disunited:

> We ought to be advancing in line with the nations of Europe and America. But the Chinese people have only family and clan groups; there is no national spirit. Consequently, in spite of four hundred million people gathered together in one China, we are in fact but a sheet of loose sand. We are the poorest and weakest state in the world, occupying the lowest position in international affairs; the rest of mankind is the carving knife and the serving dish, while we are the fish and the meat.[10]

The country's greatest challenge was its internal disunity. There was no loyalty to the larger notion of a nation. Sun continued: 'If we do not earnestly promote nationalism and weld together our four hundred millions into a strong nation, we face a tragedy – the loss of our country and the destruction of our race.'[11]

Chiang Kai-shek, as Sun's effective successor after the latter's death in 1925, continued the Nationalist Party's mission. Writing in *China's Destiny*, he declared: 'Thus the opportunity for the recovery of the nation and the hope of the rebirth of the state are now presented to the citizens of the entire country.'[12] Chiang was also keen to address what he called the country's 'moral deterioration'. The splendid legacy of a long, continuous civilized history had been degraded by the impact of outsiders in modern times. But Chinese people took ultimate responsibility for this. Foreigners had exploited weaknesses which were already present:

> The [foreign] concessions were not only the source of drugs, but were havens for prostitutes, gamblers, thieves, and bandits. When economic conditions in the interior were poor, the people migrated to the cities. But it was difficult to find employment and they were therefore forced to sell their sons and daughters and fell into the evil habits of prostitution. Thus, during the past hundred years, beautiful and prosperous cities became hells of misery and chaos.[13]

In this account, Chinese people had thus betrayed their own history and their identity and moral values.

Chiang's commitment to nationalism chimed with that of Communist leader Mao Zedong, though their diagnosis of their country's problems and how to solve them radically differed. Mao had adopted a sinified Marxist-Leninist analysis of why the country was in such poor shape after the collapse of the Qing, and how it would get out of this. Despite being from a similar background to Chiang, as the son of a reasonably well-off landlord, Mao set himself against the Confucian traditions of order and hierarchy that Chiang seemed to embrace. For Mao, these were the problem, not the solution. Marxist dialectics gave him the tools to analyse Chinese history as a story not of moral decline and victimization by foreigners, but instead of the clash between different classes internally, and the rising influence of powerful capitalist forces, many of them coming from outside actors like companies or governments. This was history with a scientific rationale, with a structure that was determined and predictable. The feudalist past was now moving towards a socialist, utopian outcome. As Mao wrote in 1939: 'The extreme poverty and backwardness of the peasants resulting from ruthless landlord exploitation and oppression is the basic reason why Chinese society remained at the same stage of socio-economic development for several thousands of years.'[14] He continued: 'The purpose of the Chinese revolution at the present stage is to change the existing colonial, semi-colonial and semi-feudal state of society, i.e. to strive for the completion of a new democratic revolution.'[15] Mao's China had a destiny, but in contrast to Chiang's vision, it was one that would be fulfilled through socialism and class struggle, not the spiritual nationalist recommitment to Confucian ethics sponsored by the Nationalist government's 'New Culture' movement of the 1930s.

Risen from the Ashes: China at War and After

The Second Sino-Japanese War (1937–45) was the most catastrophic moment in modern Chinese history. Japan's expansionism under its leaders from the 1930s was one cause. Another was the deterioration of the global economy following the Wall Street Collapse of 1929. Japan's noxious ideology of racial superiority towards neighbouring countries, particularly China, only added to the brewing conflict. From 1937, the two major countries of north-east Asia were pitched against each other in what was to be one of the most devastating wars in modern history. Before its attack on Pearl Harbor in 1941, Japan was in control of large swathes of coastal China, with a puppet regime doing its bidding installed both in the northeast in Manchuria, and in Shanghai. It had conducted penetrating campaigns in much of the countryside, encircling and destroying in a bid to annihilate any residue of opposition. The Nationalists fled to the south-western city of Chongqing, where, with US and

British assistance, they mounted at least some opposition. Their main function, however, was simply to survive. The Communists, in their remote Yan'an revolutionary base in the central northern province known today as Shaanxi, did not have the capacity or the manpower to do much more than harass and survive by guile. But in a loose coalition with the Nationalists, and employing Mao's guerrilla tactics, they proved surprisingly effective – at least as irritants to a Japan that was slowly and calamitously to discover that while it could control at least some of the cities, in the end the 'sand-like' quality of China in the countryside, where 90 per cent of people lived, proved too challenging. Stretched across the whole Asia Pacific, and now fighting against the might not just of the United States but also of Russia, Japan fell to defeat in 1945.

Mao may have been right when he said to the American reporter Edgar Snow in the 1960s that Communism would not have been ultimately successful in China without the searing experience of the Second World War.[16] But the war also resulted in more committed and focused nationalism. China had survived – just. But it had experienced first-hand with terrifying consequences the meaning of being undeveloped, weak, and disunited against a foe that was none of these things. Japan's advanced military, its strength and unity, were factors that caused China to suffer – and upon which after the war it was able to reflect. European colonial involvement with China had been destructive, but piecemeal. Britain never seriously attempted to subjugate the whole of the Chinese landmass. But in the Second Sino-Japanese War, 20 million perished and as many as 50 million were made homeless.

From 1949, the PRC vowed that never again would China be placed in this position of subjugation before an outside power, reinforcing the nationalism that had already been constructed. As Zheng Wang states in his study of the uses of historical memory in modern China,

> It is no exaggeration to say that almost all the important changes, revolutions and reforms in [the country] after 1840 [and the first Opium War] are somehow related – if not a direct response – to the national humiliation during those subsequent hundred years. . . . It is impossible, therefore, to reimagine the recent history of China without the implications of the century of humiliation; it is an integral part of the Chinese Chosenness-Myths-Trauma complex.[17]

This reached its culmination in the war. It was the moment of most brutal and final exposure to the will and power of others. Even with the conclusion of the war, the country remained troubled. After years of uneasy truce with the Communists as they had tried, together, to beat the invaders, the Nationalists returned to the unfinished business of eliminating their rivals in a Civil War from 1946. Exhausted and demoralized, however, Chiang's forces were defeated, fleeing to Taiwan, where they continued the Republic of China (which continues to exist to this day). The vision of Mao's Communist nationalism had prevailed. It now had a world to rebuild.

2

China Reconstructs
(1949–1958)

In 1949, the average life expectancy in China was just 31. Levels of literacy were 20 per cent.[1] Only 13 per cent of the population lived in cities by 1953.[2] With a population of 573 million, the per capita GDP was US$50, ten dollars less than India's.[3] But as Barry Naughton has explained, 'By 1949, China was still very poor, but development had nevertheless begun.' The legacy of the war meant this 'aided the Communist government in the execution of its socialist industrialization strategy'.[4] Mao had declared that the Chinese people were a blank sheet. And while there had been some attempts to develop China under the Nationalists during the Republican era, these supplied a base on which a massive amount needed to be built for the country to have any hope of modernizing successfully.

'In official histories,' historians Jeremy Brown and Paul G. Pickowicz argue, 'the early 1950s appear as a "golden age" of relative stability, economic recovery, and social harmony.'[5] In what some accounts portray as a honeymoon period, the Communists implemented a series of reforms, doing so with the mindset of a revolutionary force rather than a government. Private enterprises and non-governmental entities which had played some role in the period prior to 1949 were largely eradicated. The new regime faced severe challenges, however. The Korean War (1950–3) meant that the PRC was not at peace for the first years of its existence, but engaged in a conflict directly with UN forces, predominantly the United States, in the neighbouring Korean peninsula. Moreover, the impact of the Land Reform movement and early purges of intellectually and other distrusted groups from 1952 to 1953, the attempt to subjugate Tibet from 1951 to 1959, and looming clashes with the USSR, despite its initial role as a patron and development assister, also belong to a less ideal narrative.

Economic Priorities

One issue on which there was clear consensus was that China's renewal needed a sound material basis. The decision was made to achieve this by centrally controlled plans operating within a political framework supplied by the Party itself, though partly building on the template initiated by the previous Nationalist government during the war. This planning system has been characterized by historian Andrew Walder as one which was more pure than the Soviet model it was copied from.[6] The first Five-Year Plan in 1953 set a number of targets. The main priority was to ensure a high level of GDP growth. According to Chinese government data, from 1953 to 1978, GDP growth averaged 6.7 per cent annually. There is a lack of clear statistics from this era, with some saying the real figure was a more modest 4.5 per cent.[7] But there was definitely growth. Per capita levels of wealth rose from around US$200 by values varying from 13 to 1 per cent growth a year until 1961, when the calamitous impact of the Great Leap Forward (see below) and the famines resulted in a drop of over 25 per cent.[8]

The introduction of a planned economy had two main characteristics. The first was to mark a shift away from the business model of small entrepreneurial companies that had existed prior to the 1950s. China had been a country of artisan business people, largely working in small family-owned enterprises. Larger corporations and industrial companies that had characterized Western capitalism had never existed. 'The organization of large shareholders' companies, on which the development of Western capitalism was founded,' historian Marie-Claire Bergère wrote, 'implied a distinctive hierarchy and gave shareholders the right to supervise the company's management. In contrast, traditional Chinese capitalism depended upon networks of personal relations and family and geographical systems of solidarity, favouring forms of lateral communication rather than vertical hierarchies.'[9] Under Communism, the desire was for industrialization, steep increases in material living standards, and a shift away from agriculture towards manufacturing and mechanization. Mao himself referred to state capitalism, a new kind of economic model in China, when he wrote in 1953 that 'the present-day capitalist economy in China is a capitalist economy which for the most part is under the control of the People's Government.'[10]

The second feature was the emphasis on class struggle and the need to transform society more radically, innovations taken by Mao from Marxist-Leninist theory. In 'Correct Handling of Contradictions Among the People', Mao declared that the Chinese bourgeoisie, since the conversion of privately owned industrial and commercial entities in the previous year, were 'being transformed from exploiters into working people living by their own labour'. As long as they still got revenue from their enterprises, they had 'not yet cut themselves loose from the roots of exploitation'.[11] After Mao's death, the original words unpolished by his editors were finally issued. They were even more categorical: 'During past decades have the capitalists been so wise that they don't have to remould even a little? I don't think so. Even I need to remould [myself].'[12] The ensuing Great Leap Forward from 1958, aimed at accelerating the country's development and increasing the collectivization of industry and agriculture, was the tool by which to achieve this grand transformation.

Many of China's key industrial conglomerates, some of which exist in some form to this day, were founded in the 1950s during the first Five-Year Plan period. The 'Danwei' (work unit) system was set up around many of these, supplying education, kindergartens, healthcare, accommodation, work, and provision for the elderly. One of the striking features of the CPC's development over this time was the ways by which, through economic, educational, and other means, it was able to move into almost all levels of society, and all areas of life, largely enjoying a monopoly. It achieved this remarkably quickly, becoming by the end of the 1950s the sole, nationwide, uncontested source of organization and political expression. 'Society has been politicized to an unprecedented degree,' Political scientist A. Doak Barnett observed a decade later. These changes had led to 'a great expansion of the organizational apparatus of political power at all levels. . . . The regime has had to build new institutions to enable the nation's leaders not only to police the entire society, but also to manage the economy as a whole and indoctrinate the mass of the population.'[13]

Land Reform: China's Earliest Harvest of Sorrows

One of the paradoxes of Maoist politics was that despite its opposition to urban-based capitalism, and its core support coming from rural China (the urban population being then so small), the countryside was to suffer the greatest calamities. The famines in the 1960s are the most extreme example of this, with rural areas largely starved in order to feed cities. Land Reform was one of the most important political movements sponsored by the Mao government from 1949 onwards and it directly impacted on the countryside.

Mao had earlier observed abuse against exploitative landlords in his native Hunan in the 1920s, writing a famous report on this.[14] This was to frame his world-view in subsequent decades. China's countryside was the home to most people, but it was a place of pre-modernity, the epitome of the old society and the exploitation it involved.

Since ancient times, land had been a source of power and wealth. Those with land at least had security. But some had accrued large amounts, and others ended up with nothing, being no better than indentured slaves. If China was to reform, then the countryside needed to undergo revolution – and that meant addressing the inequalities of land ownership. State control needed to be introduced. As the 1950 Agrarian Reform Law stated in its preamble, the current arrangement was one of feudal exploitation by the landlord class 'and should be abolished and the system of peasant land ownership shall be introduced in order to set free the rural productive forces, develop agricultural production, and thus pave the way for China's new industrialization'.[15]

Of all the components of the Land Reform movement, before and after it was rolled out nationally, 'struggle sessions' were the most infamous. Mao had witnessed these in Hunan in 1926, theatrical events in which those under investigation were marched around the streets humiliatingly wearing tall dunce's hats emblazoned with their name. Eye-witness American farmer William Hinton observed the ethos of struggle sessions enacted against Party members through the eyes of a cadre called Hou:

> In work review meetings during the past week Comrade Hou had stressed the need to keep the movement from developing into a 'struggle' against the Party and cadres as individuals. The work time must keep in mind the real virtue of those whose records were under review. It must sustain their morale, preserve their sanity and keep alive in them that spark of courage, energy and ability which had made them leaders in the past.[16]

A similar need for judiciousness was necessary when landowners were exposed and had to submit to discipline and public correction. Hinton does refer obliquely to violence in his account. But other testimony shows that violence was not an unfortunate, occasional outcome of this movement, but a core part of it. Mao had been the proponent of revolution being a necessarily violent event. It was not, as he famously declared, a dinner party. Violence was inevitable and ubiquitous. The Land Reform movement was to see as many as 2 million perish, with countless other acts of physical violence against those targeted. 'Under the new guidelines of "not correcting excesses prematurely" the aroused masses frequently engaged in unchecked outbreaks of violence and brutality.'[17] It was the first widescale campaign which created a new class in the PRC – disgruntled victims – and a new elite – the middle peasants who had benefited from the redistribution. China's renewal and regeneration, as shown by this example from the very dawn of the PRC, was to be a process in which there were always clear winners and losers, and in which compromise and consensus were never easy, nor, perhaps, even the objective.

Cleansing of the People

As early as 1957, American psychologist Robert J. Lifton was able to record the 'sixiang gaizao' (thought reform) for which increasing evidence was emerging within the PRC. The aim was therefore clearly to remake not just the physical world of the Chinese people, but the inner one too. This showed the radical difference between the Communists and the Nationalists they had defeated. They had a new vision of what a Chinese person should be, and of the techniques that needed to be used in order to achieve this. According to Lifton, this consisted of confessions, in which individuals in writing or in public recounted the deeds they had done in the old world, before the regime came into existence, and the sins they had committed. With this act completed, they were able to move on to a programme of re-education.[18]

'Thought reform' was about accepting a collectivist ethos, 'serving the people', and accepting broad social responsibilities in the great project the country was now embarked on to restore and regenerate itself.

People were either for or against this. There was no space in-between. Nor was the Party immune from this process of self-reformation and self-inspection. It, too, was targeted by campaigns in order to improve the posture of cadres. They were to be not just administrators, but part of a new model moral army. The selfishness of the past, what Mao complained was the parochialism of 'mountain stronghold' ideas (*shantou zhuyi*), needed to be eradicated.

Practically, that meant an end to prostitution and other vices associated with capitalism and the previous regime. It meant that foot binding, a practice introduced in the imperial era that effectively crippled young women, was outlawed. It meant the provision of mass education, and a set menu of ideological messages delivered not just to Party members, but to the whole of society. It meant destroying the sorts of inequalities that manifested themselves in cities in terms of what kind of housing people lived in. Peasants had their lands redistributed and city workers had apartments and sets of rooms reallocated and reassigned.

Intellectuals figured importantly in this. To understand the particular quality of animosity that Mao evidently felt towards this group, one has to remember that the term in Chinese – '*zhishi fenzi*' – literally translates as 'knowledge elements'. This covered a far wider group than the same term in English, running from teachers to those who worked in journalism, and who could be more broadly categorized as service sector workers in Western systems. That accounted for a sizeable number of people. Mao's own history with this group had also been a difficult one. 'Mao had long found intellectuals irritating,' Alexander Pantsov and Stephen Levine wrote in their biography of the Chairman. 'Skeptical and conscientious, they aroused in him, as well as in other Bolshevik leaders, hatred and revulsion.'[19] This may have derived from Mao's early life, when, as a lowly librarian at Beijing University, he had experienced first-hand the sharp treatment and intimidating behaviour those serving intellectuals sometimes suffered.

Despite this, 'knowledge elements' were important to the new China, as engineers, medical practitioners, and planners. In terms of the social background of its leadership, the CPC was from humble stock. But now that it was in government, it needed those conversant in science, maths, and technology to be able to devise and implement its macro-economic and political plans. The issue with intellectuals, which would never be dispelled in the Maoist era, and lingers to this day, is that they were likely to be complicated in their private thoughts and allegiance. Some of them had studied abroad, in the pre-1949 period when young Chinese went to Japan, Europe, and the United States to study. Others were linked to family members who had fled with the Nationalists to Taiwan. Some were simply dissenters, aware of the creed of Marxism but also equipped to critique and doubt it. This group had to be reshaped somehow. 'Thought reform' was initially the means to do this.

Writer Yang Jiang (1911–2016) typifies the fate of many of this group. A formidable intellect, she had studied with her husband, scholar Qian Zhongshu (1910–98), in Oxford and then the Sorbonne in the 1930s. In 1947, in *Cities Besieged* (*Wei Cheng*), Qian had produced one of the best-loved novels of the life of those exposed to overseas culture and carrying their experiences back to their home country. Yang's own work largely consisted of producing the first translations into Chinese of works like *Don Quixote* by Cervantes. She also wrote plays, criticism, and a series of memoirs. Living back in the new China, she and her husband were seen by the PRC government as a propaganda opportunity – a sign to others still abroad to return and do as this couple had, contributing to the creation of a new society – but also a target of persistent distrust and wariness. This created the environment of perpetual ambiguity that surrounded Yang and others like her.

In the 1980s, Yang wrote her sole novel, *Xizao*, whose English translation, *Baptism*, loses some of its clear reference to the idea of 'cleansing', as in the Chinese *xinao* (brainwashing). It referred back to the very early period when intellectuals, some of them returnees, were sent to staff the recently founded Social Science Institutes. A group of these individuals experience complex shifts and transformations in their relationships. Some of this is the result of the differences in their professional backgrounds before being brought together by government edict. Some is the result of personal issues between them. It is noticeable that throughout the novel Yang spends a lot of attention describing the clothes that people wear, and the ways that while these change and transform, fundamental character traits are evidently not so easy to eradicate. The novel obliquely, and critically, refers to the above-mentioned 'thought reform' movement happening at the time. And the ending is one laden with ambiguity, with two of the key characters tiptoeing around an affair, but then, frozen by their marital obligations, having to renounce their passions and endure their current situation.[20] That stands as a fair metaphor for the relationship between intellectuals generally and the Party by the mid-1950s: mutually reliant, and yet also mutually distrustful and each devising ways of trying to manage their lives with each other.

China and the World

Nor were the enemies solely within. New China after its establishment was an isolated place. The Nationalists, in fleeing to the island of Taiwan, also took with them most diplomatic alliances, including that with the United States, and a seat on the newly established United Nations. The Republic of China, with less than 5 per cent of the land mass of the PRC, and only a fraction of the people (in 1949, its population came to 7 million), was seen as the 'real China'. Mao's country was simply regarded as an interloper.

For the USSR and its allies, however, the similarity in political model meant that they did have to confer recognition. The PRC was formally established on 1 October 1949. The USSR recognized it the next day. The Democratic People's Republic of Korea (i.e. North Korea) followed five days later. But by the end of 1949, there were still only twelve states recognizing Beijing. By 1960, the PRC only increased its quota of countries with formal links by twenty-two.

Alliance with the USSR was perhaps the most significant move that the PRC government made in international affairs at its foundation. 'The [CPC's] decision to ally with the Soviet Union was a major factor spreading Cold War conflict in East Asia,' John Garver has written in a comprehensive diplomatic history of this period. 'The PRC's decision to ally with the Soviet Union had a profound impact on China's foreign relations and on the entire world situation.'[21] Dependence on Moscow for technical and financial assistance was one element of this. So was Mao's quest to maintain the uniqueness and autonomy of the new country's position. In many ways, the Five Principles of Peaceful Coexistence that Foreign Minister Zhou Enlai (1898–1976) announced at the conference in Bandung, Indonesia, in 1955, with their premium placed on non-interference in the affairs of others and respect for their sovereignty, were aimed at protecting the PRC as much from Russian influence as from that of the imperialist capitalist West.

If Chinese Communism had grown from the soil

of the Russian Revolution, it certainly did not feel beholden to it. While Stalin was alive, Mao was respectful. But after his death in 1953 the first sign of cracks started to appear. The most costly issue for Beijing as it created its new network of international relations was the decision by fellow socialist nation North Korea in 1950 to attack the South, from which it had been divided as a result of the outcome of the Second World War. Kim Il Sung had spent many years in north-east China. Chinese Communism, with its hybridity, had clearly had a profound impact on him. But his own version proved as bespoke as that practised in Beijing, with a fierce focus on Korean nationalism. The cost of Kim's attack on South Korea under US protection was to be high for Mao. It not only included the loss of his own son along with up to a million other troops, but also provided a deeply unwanted distraction from the unfinished business of Taiwan. Deployment of over 3 million soldiers across the Yalu river into North Korea meant that at a crucial time when planning had already proceeded to see the People's Liberation Army (PLA) make moves across the Taiwan Strait to take on the Nationalists on the island, everything was halted. The PRC had a small window of opportunity to effect its unification plans. North Korea effectively scuppered these. By the time of the announcement of the ceasefire in 1953, America had already solidified its alliance with Taiwan. The situation, in Beijing's eyes at least, remains unresolved to this day.

3

The Years of Dissent
(1958–1966)

From 1958 to the start of the Cultural Revolution (CR) a decade later, the new republic was beset by a series of internal and external challenges. Of the external, the most significant by far was the schism with the USSR. Domestically, the impact of this was to drive China under Mao towards greater economic self-sufficiency, but also to cause the dominance of the political over all other objectives. Some of this was perhaps a pragmatic response to the isolated situation in which China found itself. It had no other choice but to be self-reliant. Even so, from the late 1950s, there was a greater focus on class struggle, escalating social mobilization through mass campaigns, and the emergence of competing factions and viewpoints within the Party itself, and between it and Mao. The Hundred Flowers campaign of 1957, when intellectuals and others were invited by the Party to express their views of how things were going, seemed to presage a period of liberalism and openness. But it was swiftly closed down when criticism became too sharp, and was followed by the fervour of the Great Leap Forward, the disastrous impact of which led, in the early 1960s, to the most tragic period of PRC history: the terrible famines until 1962. The price for these was Mao's temporary sidelining and the first appearance of a softer form of renewal and reform through the Four Modernizations spearheaded by Liu Shaoqi (1898–1969) as President and Deng Xiaoping (1904–97) as Secretary General of the Party. A resentful Mao, however, was to emerge in 1966 even more zealously convinced that his radical programme was the right one to deliver the goal desired by all: a strong, powerful country.

The Sino-Soviet Split

Mao's relationship with the Soviet Communist Party and its international brand, the Comintern, had always been a turbulent one. Moscow-trained revolutionaries like Li Lisan or Wang Ming were eventually purged in rectification campaigns during Mao's rise to power in the 1930s and 1940s. Stalin's support for the Chinese Communists in the crucial period from the end of the Second World War to 1949 had been highly equivocal. He had taken a view to be found in the words of Marx himself that China was simply not the right location for constructing a socialist country, and that its lack of a proper proletariat meant it should have a supporting rather than a lead role in the global struggle for social and political transformation.

Despite this, Mao was respectful of Stalin at their meetings during his two visits to the USSR. Indeed, the USSR was the only foreign country Mao ever visited. Moscow observed the niceties of its responsibility to its junior partner in revolution, giving it material support in the early years of the PRC. China figured as a little brother in its world-view, a perspective tinged with a sense of cultural and economic superiority. The death of Stalin in 1953 did not immediately precipitate a crisis. But the emergence of the new leadership meant that by 1956 relations were cooling. That they broke down entirely was largely to do with the process of de-Stalinization precipitated by the secret talk at the 1956 congress in which new General Secretary Khrushchev denounced his predecessor and ushered in a period of liberalization. Stalin's dictatorial, autocratic decision-making manner and the cult of personality were particular targets for disapprobation. This was the aspect that most concerned Mao, because there were plenty of parallels with his style of leadership. This is unsurprising because of the ways the structures of power in the PRC had been broadly copied from the USSR. Within the next three years Soviet experts were withdrawn from China, and relations entered a period of sharp deterioration. By 1969, the two were effectively at war, with a nasty, brief clash on their north-eastern border. The era of China's isolation had started.

Liberalization with Maoist Characteristics

In the summer of 1956, almost at the same time as Khrushchev was making his secret speech, Mao had discussed with his fellow leaders the need to create

greater discussion and more inclusivity in the Party.
His real motives have remained controversial to this
day. Whether the encouragement of open criticism was
a way of exposing enemies hidden within, or simply
a well-intended plan that went wrong because of the
strength of the feelings expressed once space was created for them, it was clear from comments made by
Mao at the time that he was wary of what he saw as
the creeping bureaucratization of the Party – and of its
potential annexation by intellectuals and other forces.
Mao remained a romantic revolutionary, an outsider
even in his own Party, and someone who deliberately
celebrated the power of contradictions and inconsist-
ency. 'The unity of opposites, hard fighting, and rest
and consolidation, is a law,' he had declared in 1958
in the south-western city of Chengdu.

> There is nothing which does not undergo such trans-
> formation. 'Haste' is transformed into 'deliberation',
> and 'deliberation' is transformed into 'haste'. . . . It is
> the same with rest and consolidation and hard fight-
> ing. Toil and dreams, deliberation and haste, also have
> [an element of] identity; rest and consolidation and
> hard fighting also have an element of identity. Going
> to bed and getting up is also a unity of opposites.[1]

Fittingly, for the proponent of such a philosophy,
there are at least two Maos. The Mao of his official
published material is polished, controlled, and well
presented. This voice figures in the *Selected Works*

in Chinese and English published over the decades. But there is the Mao who was extempore, talking off the cuff – the figure whose voice we find in the vast amounts of material produced particularly during the CR, when it was popular to issue words he was reported to have delivered at meetings, in informal settings. This Mao is rough, frequently disjointed, and much more troublesome. As this second Mao declared in 1959, at a moment of particular crisis when his leadership was being questioned: 'The chaos caused was on a grand scale and I take responsibility. Comrade, you must all analyse your own responsibility. If you have to shit, shit! If you have to fart, fart! You will feel much better for it.'[2] The question is not so much which was the real Mao – in some senses, both were two aspects of the same thing. It is more what was the relationship between these two figures in one political persona, and, at any particular time, which had the upper hand: the formal Mao, crafted and tamed by his minders and courtiers, or the earthy Mao, connecting directly with people, and speaking a language more akin to their world. The Hundred Flowers campaign shows an elision between these two: Mao as conciliatory, consensus building, statesmanlike, to be quickly replaced by the Mao of invective, vengeance, and fury.

A history of this period written using source material that consisted wholly of the voice of the second Mao would be a very different kind in tone and implication from one which stuck to the polished Mao of his formally issued announcements. It has only been through the assiduous work of scholars like Stuart Schram and Roderick MacFarquhar that the latter Mao has seen the light of day, at least for English-speaking audiences. The second Mao was unambiguous in his attitude towards intellectuals, which implies that from the start the Hundred Flowers campaign and its invitation for open discussion was not likely to end well. 'Professors,' he declared after the campaign ended, 'we have been afraid of them ever since we came into the towns. We did not despise them, we were terrified of them. When confronted by people with piles of learning we felt we were good for nothing. For Marxists to fear bourgeois intellectuals, to fear professors while not fearing imperialism, is strange indeed.'[3] His conclusion was unequivocal. 'We must not tolerate it any longer.' In 1957, Mao had spoken with literary and art circles. Once more, his antagonism towards the very people he was addressing was palpable. 'Only by identifying with the workers, peasants and soldiers can [one] have a way out. [If you] can't identify with [them], what can you write about?' He went on, 'If [the writers] don't go on to identify with the workers, peasants and soldiers . . . what can you do?'[4] Even in the midst of the campaign, for all the stress on diversity and encouraging a carnival atmosphere of varying opinions and perspectives, Mao was clear about the ultimate objective: 'The Communist Party . . . wants to move things along, unify thinking, have a common language. Otherwise,' he explained, '[when] you say [it's] bureaucratism, he says [it's] not. You say, "Let a hundred flowers bloom, let a hundred schools contend," he says, don't bloom. [When we] bloom a bit, and there are some bad results, [they] start running around in circles.'[5]

Mao's position, and the clarity of his objective, meant he could enunciate these kinds of criticisms. But some of the voices that started to come from the liberalization movement were increasingly unwelcome. Liu Binyan (1925–2005), a journalist based in Beijing for the *Beijing Youth News*, was to respond by writing a series of short stories and articles. One, 'Inside News', has a non-Party member, Huang Jiaying, articulate a complaint that was made by many others:

> The problem [in the Party] is more serious than too many meetings. Look at what they are about and you'll understand. The most trivial things have to go through all the layers of the bureaucracy and be repeatedly discussed. Then everyone had to be mobilized several times and give promises to fulfill targets. That's not to mention the extra meetings, first for Party members and then for League members, and first for the cadres, then for the masses. A miner who is a Party member often has to go to seven or eight meetings on the same subject. Since 1952, the workers have been saying that meetings are more tiring than work; they'd rather do overtime. And everyone has to say something at the meetings even if they have nothing to say.[6]

There was nothing striking about this declaration – apart from the fact that something so unsurprising and unradical could be problematic to state overtly. Liu was swept up in the anti-rightist movement – the clampdown after the Hundred Flowers campaign was abruptly called to a halt – and had to undergo 'thought reform'. At least he was allowed to return to work in Beijing in 1961. For figures like the friend of Lu Xun, Zhang Guangren (1902–85), who went under the pen name Hu Feng, their ordeal was to be longer, and more harrowing. Branded part of a counter-revolutionary clique as early as 1955, and sent for reform and re-education the following year, for over a decade he was unable to see his wife or his children, but was incarcerated in the infamous Qincheng Prison close to Beijing. In his wife's moving account of these years, published posthumously, she recalls a meeting between the two in the mid-1960s. Hu Feng had declared:

> Was I wrong to study Marxism-Leninism? I loyally followed the Party, everything I did was for the Party, was that wrong too? Of course, I know the secret of how to survive under a big hat, but is that being responsible to the Party and the people? Or to oneself? Is that what I should do? I can't admit to things I haven't done and whether what I have done is wrong or not can't be answered in one sentence.[7]

Hu's internal conflict was not uncommon. For many of those caught up in the anti-rightist clampdown, the worst sufferings were those their conscience inflicted on them. They believed in the project to recreate their country, and many of them had even returned from abroad in order to contribute. They wanted to be loyal – but clearly did not know what precisely they were meant to be loyal to. In the abstract, the aims of Mao and the Party were ones they could accept. What was problematic was the means of getting there, and the idea of what in the end the realization of this great utopian dream in detail might mean. Hu himself was finally released in the late 1970s, and lived for a few years in freedom. But his wife's account makes it clear that to the end he was a prisoner of Mao's complex demands and the capricious way that these had been enforced. There was the Party, and there was Mao. And while they had reasonable concord at least during the 1950s, by the end of this period they were increasingly at odds with each other. It was the Great Leap Forward that was to bring this to breaking point.

Going to the Moon: The Great Leap Forward

Mao's nationalism was not generically different to versions that have raised their head since his era, either in China or elsewhere. China was a great country. The intellectuals and others, with their lack of both confidence and faith, had been exposed and dealt with. The policy response was simply to accelerate the planned economy, the setting up of communes, and the implementation of the great vision to see a country freed of victimization, powerful, confident, and strong, emerge from all the challenges that had been thrown at it.

'Now,' Mao declared in early 1958, 'our enthusiasm has been aroused. Ours is an ardent nation, now swept by a burning tide. There is a good metaphor for this: our nation is like an atom. . . . When this atom's nucleus is smashed, the thermal energy released will have really tremendous power.' That power would manifest itself in spectacular industrialization and material growth. 'We shall be able to do things which we could not do before. When our nation has this energy we shall catch up with Britain in fifteen years. . . . We must summon up our strength and swim vigorously upstream.'[8] The objective of the Great Leap Forward is well enough known: establishing throughout the country communes which were required to engage in industrial output. Backyard furnaces were one manifestation of this, making poor-quality steel which only satisfied statistical demands, and had no proper practical use. The Great Leap Forward, in the words of Franz Schurmann, was 'a vision, not a plan'.[9] Its outcome was 'a massive increase in the rate at which resources were transferred from agriculture to industry'.[10] What was left of the free market was eliminated. Decision-making was decentralized. Good harvests in 1958 and increases in productivity initially gave the impression that China was on the right track. However, overreporting of results back to the centre by cadres eager to show they were contributing to success meant a false sense of security was created. Disastrously, the shift away from supporting agriculture, and the all-out commitment to industrialization, meant that the foundation for the catastrophe of the coming years was laid. Poor weather conditions only exacerbated this. The worst famines suffered by any society in the twentieth century, and perhaps in the whole of human history, were the real legacy of the Great Leap. Another was to create an even deeper rift between Mao, the Party, and the people. This was to shape the ensuing two decades.

Death in the Countryside: The Great Famines

Even in the twenty-first century, candour about the impact and extent of the famines remains limited. Arguments about the number of deaths and the culpability for the famines continues. The 1981 'Resolution on certain questions in the history of our party since the founding of the People's Republic of China', issued by the Central Committee, the most formal assessment by the CPC of its own history produced in the post-Mao era, consigned the whole event to a single sentence: 'It was mainly due to the errors of the Great Leap Forward and of the struggle against "Right opportunism" together with a succession of natural calamities and the perfidious scrapping of contracts by the Soviet Government,' the document stated, 'that our economy encountered serious difficulties between 1959 and 1961, which caused serious losses to our country and people.'[11] No statistics are given; blame was simply apportioned to the outside world, and to internal enemies. It is easy to understand how this kind of historiography means that when scholars like Yang Jisheng produced a painstaking account in the late 2000s, their work created consternation, and in some quarters outright denial.

Part of the power of Yang's work is the enormous amount of data he is able to produce to support his arguments and estimates. As a journalist for Xinhua, the PRC's official news agency, he had what previous writers about this event did not: access to official statistics and documents.[12] With this, he was able to state that over the three years of the famine 36 million had perished. There had also been a significant drop in the birth rate. 'How can we conceptualize the 36 million people who starved to death?,' Yang asks in the preamble to his book *Tombstone*, part-testament, part-memorial to these horrifying events. 'This number is equivalent to 450 times the number of people killed by the atomic bomb on Nagasaki.' The manner of their death was the most shocking thing. 'There were no anguished appeals to heaven, no hemp-robed funerals, no firecrackers and hell money to see the departed to their final destination, no sympathy, nor grief, no tears, no shock, no dread. Tens of millions departed this world in an atmosphere of mute apathy.'[13] Moving from the central province of Henan, out to Gansu in the north-west, then to Anhui, another central province, Yang documents in painstaking detail the scale of the catastrophe, the inadequacy of the response of officials, and the initial bemusement finally disintegrating to panic in Beijing.

There were consequences within the Party, and the appearance of a schism between Mao and the very people he had led to power. His Defence Minister, Peng Dehuai (1898–1974), was the most outspoken. On a visit to the countryside, Peng had witnessed some of the emerging hardship in 1959. Attending a top-level Party conference that year in Lushan in Jiangxi province, one of the early centres of Communist power, he had dared to voice his concerns. Mao was to take this personally. 'The first Lushan Conference of 1959 was originally concerned with work,' Mao complained a year later. 'Then up jumped [Peng] and said "You fucked my mother for forty days, can't I fuck your mother for twenty days?" All this fucking messed up the conference and the work was affected.'[14] Peng was initially sidelined. In the CR he was effectively hounded to death. But his point was an effective one. From the early 1960s, Mao was himself reduced to a peripheral position, maintaining what was intended to be a ceremonial and symbolic role as Chairman, but largely uninvolved with day-to-day governance affairs. That was left to the President, Liu Shaoqi, and his very capable deputy, Deng Xiaoping.

The most unpalatable aspect of the whole period was the brute fact that the countryside, home to the revolution in the early years, had been starved in order to continue to feed the cities. The farmers and rural

dwellers who had been the most faithful support-
ers of Communism had been sacrificed as a result of
poor policy- and decision-making by the very people
they had brought to power. The Chinese countryside
was always a little-understood place, with its dense
network of different relationships and clan alliances.
Some of these maintained antipathies and hierarchies
that reached back centuries. War, civil war, the Land
Reform programme, and then the dislocation from
the Great Leap Forward and the famines had made
matters worse. At the front line from 1949 were local
Party officials, those who were the foot soldiers for
the great revolution for renewal who were to enact the
Maoist programme at the most local level. But by the
early 1960, levels of trust had been eroded to such an
extent that there was a situation akin almost to war.
In his seminal study of relations between officials and
farmers in Da Fo, a village in northern Henan over
the period prior to and after the Great Leap Forward,
American scholar Ralph Thaxton describes a host of
different strategies whereby villagers were able to try
to circumvent diktats by the Party, and ways that the
Party officials tried to hit back. 'The voices of Da Fo
villagers tell us that during the Great Leap, the Maoists
institutionalized forms of structural coercion and corruption that ruined villagers . . . [and] left a legacy
of bitter memories as well as an arsenal of weapons
of coping and resistance that survived through various previously hidden processes of transmission.'[15]
Thaxton uses the memorable phrase 'whispered his-

tories' to capture this: the memory of the unsayable through silent testimony – a testimony that would one day be uttered and on which action would be taken.

The ethos of the Great Leap Forward, whatever its aftermath, is not so easy to dismiss. The Maoist-inspired tactics which were used to achieve the grand vision may have been utterly wrong, but the underlying objective remained unchanged. In many ways, the same kind of eagerness to move ahead quickly, and impatience to see things happen faster, were to typify much of what followed. Nor was it entirely safe to assume, as leaders like Liu and Deng did during the years of Mao's sidelining, that conferring on him solely symbolic power would neutralize him. It was precisely this kind of power that he was the great genius at manipulating. This was something they would learn, to their great expense, from 1966 onwards.

Four Modernizations: Their First Appearance

By 1962, relations had deteriorated so badly with the Soviet Union that an official declaration from the Party could declare 'Khrushchev's "communism" is indeed "goulash communism", the "communism of the American way of life" and "communism seeking credits from the devil.'[16] As a symbol of its ability to go it alone, in October 1964, at the Lop Nur site in Xinjiang, Beijing successfully tested a nuclear bomb. 'This is a major achievement of the Chinese people in their struggle to increase their national defense capability and oppose the United States imperialist policy of nuclear blackmail and nuclear threats,' a statement issued by Xinhua declared the next day. It went on:

> The Chinese Government will, as always, exert every effort to promote the realization of the noble aim of the complete prohibition and thorough destruction of nuclear weapons through international consultations. Before the advent of such a day, the Chinese Government and people will firmly and unswervingly march along their own road of strengthening their national defenses, defending their motherland and safeguarding world peace.[17]

Despite the lofty rhetoric, it was clear that having the bomb suited China's image as a powerful country, and one that could now claim it belonged to the select group of great powers, even if it did not yet have a seat on the United Nations. In 1967, it was to follow up with a hydrogen bomb test. Nuclear technology development was one of the protected areas during the CR, off-limits even during the most chaotic periods to disruptive Red Guard groups and their activities.

The bomb would not have been created, or at least not as quickly, without the significant assistance, before they formally departed, of Soviet experts. But China was clearly in a more bellicose mood over this period, launching a brief but effective border war against India, which it won in 1962 (and which remains the source of bad feeling between the two great neighbours to this day, with the border still the subject of bitter dispute). Relations with India had been vastly complicated by the fleeing of the Dalai Lama there from Tibet during what was in effect its annexation in 1959.

Domestically, however, the pre-CR era saw a very early attempt to adopt more pragmatic, moderate policies, after having learned the lessons of the Great Leap Forward and the disastrous aftermath of this. In December 1964, Premier Zhou Enlai had for the first time enunciated the concept of the Four Modernizations: 'The major task for developing our national economy in the years to come is, in brief, to turn China into a powerful socialist country with modern agriculture, modern industry, modern national defence and modern science and technology.' Zhou, as ever, was the acme of harmonious balance. 'We must do better in applying the guiding principles of economic development, namely, that agriculture is the foundation and industry the leading factor.' There could be no more onslaughts on the countryside. Things needed to be done with proper sequencing and sustainably. In a line that would not have looked amiss in a leader's speech half a century later, he continued, 'It is necessary to bring out people's ingenuity and talent into full play and to carry out extensive experiments. We must absorb all the good experiences and technologies of other countries, learning from other countries must be combined with creativity on our own part.'[18] Liu Shaoqi and Deng Xiaoping had toyed with ideas in rural areas allowing farmers to sell grain to the local brigade for a small profit after fulfilling a pre-agreed quota.[19] The success of pilot schemes for this meant that 20 per cent of farmers were enrolled by 1962.[20] This went hand in hand with a concerted campaign of de-Maoification, in which Mao's supreme position in the Party was criticized at events like the 7000 cadres conference in 1962, where fellow leaders like Peng Zhen (1902–97) and Liu himself had seemed to directly contest his position.[21] Mao's brooding throughout this period was ominous, but simply accepted as more indicative of short-term sulking than the signs of someone nursing a profound desire for vengeance.

4

The Great Proletariat Cultural Revolution (1966–1976)

The Great Proletariat Cultural Revolution (CR), to give it its formal name, was launched in mid-1966. In one form or another it was to dominate the ensuing decade. It was only to end when Mao Zedong himself died in September 1976, though by that time much of the original energy and purpose propelling this, the most significant and epic of all the mass mobilization campaigns in PRC history, had dissipated. To outsiders, even today, after so much has been written about this period, it remains often bewildering. What precisely was it? An intra-elite political struggle for dominance by one group over the other? An idealistic but misguided attempt to finally purge China of the influence of its stultifying Confucian legacy? A working out of deep divisions, resentments, and conflicts within a society both in the countryside and in the cities which was complicated, fragmented, and traumatized after the famines and the Great Leap Forward, something akin to a mass public nervous breakdown? In essence, it was all of these things – along with some that related to China's relations with the outside world. But one thing is certain. Without Mao Zedong, there would have been no such movement. It is stamped with his love of contradiction, his capriciousness, and the unique hybridity of his thinking.

Certainly, at its genesis, the CR had grand ambitions. It was, according to the CPC Central Committee, 'a great revolution that touches people to their very souls and constitutes a new development of the socialist revolution in our country'.[1] In the *People's Daily*, the official Party newspaper, the rallying call was even more impassioned: 'With the tremendous and impetuous force of a raging storm, [workers, peasants, and soldiers] have smashed the shackles imposed on their minds by the exploiting classes for so long in the past.'[2] The era even saw the creation of its own sub-dialect, a language rich in invective, and conducted as much by slogans as by actions, where words were deeds, and huge daubed slogans were strung in boards across the countryside, or fixed to city walls. The characters for people's names were inscribed forcefully on hoardings which were then strung around the neck of targets, crossed through in red ink. Ren Zhongyi, provincial Party Secretary of Harbin in the north-east Heilongjiang province, was one such target, captured by photographer Li Zhensheng around 1967, head crowned with a huge paper dunce's cap, standing on a wooden chair before a massive crowd denouncing him, the placard hung on him declaring him to be a 'black gang element', his face smeared with ink.[3] The CR drew on traditions of peasant protest that Mao had observed in his native Hunan in the 1920s (see Chapter 2). It also drew on language forms that reached back into the very distant past and on traditional culture the whole movement ostensibly was meant to be decrying – with its castigation of 'cow ghosts and snake demons', an old Buddhist curse, and the invective against groups like intellectuals ('stinking number nines')[4] and the imperial emperors, labels given to Party Secretaries in provinces regarded as becoming over-mighty.

Bombard the Headquarters

The principal target of the CR, for a Mao who had been criticized and sidelined by the disastrous outcome of the Great Leap Forward, was the Party itself, and, in particular, elements in the upper levels of the leadership. These were accused of following the revisionist path of the detested Soviet Union, now under the leadership of Brezhnev. 'It is right to rebel,' Mao had declared in Yan'an, in the 1940s.[5] Repeated *ad nauseam* in the 1960s, it was supplemented by plentiful denunciations of Party officials and their attitude by Mao himself. 'They are conceited, complacent and they aimlessly discuss politics,' he complained of some cadres in 1970. 'Their bureaucratic attitude is immense . . . they are ignorant . . . they do not understand politics.'[6] The list went on: negligence, stupidity, egotism, selfishness, and disunity. This culture of indolence had been created and instilled by figures like Liu Shaoqi and Deng Xiaoping. These, and others like Peng Zhen, Bo Yibo, and Peng Dehuai, were to figure as major targets of the CR onslaught. But for that, Mao needed his own parallel institutional structures and people to implement this.

For institutions, Mao supported the establishment of Cultural Revolutionary Groups, Committees, and Congresses. These lay outside the formal Party structures but shadowed and paralleled them. 'These cultural revolutionary groups, committees and organizations are excellent new forms of organization whereby the masses educate themselves under the leadership of the Communist Party,' the formal decision announcing their existence in May 1966 stated.[7] Despite the harmonious language about 'leadership' by the Party, in fact these groups were often directly antagonistic to it. Of these new entities, the Central Cultural Revolution Group, set up from a brief predecessor entity, the Five Man Group, was key. This brought in figures who in the coming years would play key roles in the development of the CR, the most significant among them being Chen Boda (1904–89), a writer and editor for Mao since his early career; Jiang Qing (1914–91), Mao's fourth wife; Kang Sheng (c.1898–1975), his greatly feared head of internal intelligence; and Zhang Chunqiao (1917–2005), a writer mostly active in Shanghai. The group was disbanded and replaced with military and other revolutionary committees because of its association in 1967 with events like the Wuhan Incident (in which the military had to quell clashing radical groups) and the Shanghai February Counter-Current (a fight between different factions claiming to be loyal to Mao). Both of these events almost led to civil war. Nevertheless, the rebellious ethos instilled from this early period did not vanish, and the leadership of the Central Cultural Revolution Group appeared in different guises but engaged in the same kinds of incitement and trouble-making.[8]

Supplementing these were the dreaded Red Guard Groups, seemingly spontaneously set up as schools and colleges started to wind down over 1966. As Andrew Walder has pointed out, however, 'The red guard movement, of course, did not emerge spontaneously. It was initiated and encouraged by China's highest political authorities.'[9] That meant, in effect, Mao. Red Guards figure as key parts of the *dramatis personae* of the CR. Establishing liaison stations on an almost military-style basis, dressed in distinctive clothes (the Sun Yat-sen suit favoured by Mao, adorned with red armbands), it was mostly personnel from these who filled Tiananmen Square during the vast million-strong rallies over 1966 into 1967 when they were allowed to have sight of the Chairman, 'the reddest reddest sun in their hearts'. One such fervent Mao worshipper, Bei Guancheng, writing in 1967, recorded his participation in a rally that year:

Finally, I managed to get to the visitor's stand, and by a stroke of luck just then Chairman Mao came over to the east side of the rostrum. I could see him ever so clearly, and he was so impressive. Comrades, how can I possibly describe to you what that moment was like? In any case, I together with everyone else just exploded in shouts of 'Long Live Chairman Mao!' Having seen Chairman Mao, I made a silent pledge to definitely become Chairman Mao's good pupil.[10]

With these two principal groups – the Central Cultural Revolution Group and the myriad of different Red Guard factional entities – Mao had the infrastructure in place to mount what was almost a counter-insurgency. The core elite targets for his ire were the President in 1966, Liu Shaoqi, and his closest associate, Deng Xiaoping. While not referred to directly, at least in the early months of the campaign, it became blatantly clear that it was these who were being singled out when fiery language appeared in Red Guard pamphlets stencilled and printed through late 1966 to 1967 obsessively attacking 'the key persons in power taking the capitalist road'. 'Capitalist roaders' was the core label of abuse, though it was supplemented by coruscating language about 'Soviet revisionists'. Liu's sidelining and removal was amongst the most brutal acts in Mao's long career. Proxy agents from Red Guard groups were allowed to enter the sacred leadership compound of Zhongnanhai in Beijing next to the Forbidden Palace and humiliate a man still regarded till then as the Chairman's most likely successor. Deng Xiaoping was forced to produce a grovelling self-criticism before the Central Committee of the Party in October 1966. 'I have not raised high the great banner of Mao Zedong Thought, nor have I followed Chairman Mao closely,' he said. 'I cut myself off from the leadership, in addition my contact with the masses is infrequent and I am isolated from reality. . . . Recent events have revealed me as an unreformed petit-bourgeoisie intellectual who has failed to pass the test.'[11] Liu was to be exiled to the central city of Kaifeng, where he died in 1969 of untreated cancer. Deng survived, sent initially to work in a tractor factory in southern Jiangxi province in the early 1970s, and was then rehabilitated in 1974, and, once more after Mao's death, this time for good, in 1978.

Smashing the Four Olds

The chief impetus to renew and renovate China for the CR movement did not come from the intra-elite political fights in Beijing. These were little different from fights between different political groups in the past. The main rejuvenating idea was to cleanse society of the heavy burden of history. 'Smash the Four Olds' – namely old customs, culture, habits, and ideas – was one aspect of this. The other was the specifically cultural work of the whole vast movement: the eight revolutionary operas sponsored by Mao's wife, the radical Jiang Qing, for instance, and the attempt to fully implement the socialist 'literature and art for the masses' line that had first appeared during the Yan'an era in the 1940s. Finally there was the 'Criticize Lin

Biao, Criticize Confucius' movement in the early 1970s (see below).

The CR ostensibly had started with an argument over literature – at least, over the meaning of the metaphors and symbols and their true target in a play by a Vice-Mayor of Beijing, Wu Han (1909–69). Wu's play was about the dismissal hundreds of years before by an emperor of the faithful official Hai Rui. Radicals claimed that this was an oblique reference to the argument between Mao (the emperor) and Peng Dehuai (the official Hai Rui) in 1959. Wu was to be one of the chief targets of the CR in its early phase, dying in prison in 1969. The CR embraced a modernization of cultural production and its mass dissemination. It developed the kinds of revolutionary operas and artistic innovations made in the earlier Yan'an period of the Party's existence before it came to power. During this period it championed formats and content that expanded the audience for Chinese culture away from the elitist, highly literate, exclusive, and excluding constituency that had enjoyed, consumed, and produced material before the modern era.

Jiang Qing was key in all of this. An actress before her marriage to Mao in the 1930s, she had disappeared from view through most of the post-1949 period, but re-emerged with a vengeance when the CR started. Her chief 'hired pen' was the polemicist Yao Wenyuan (1931–2005), like Jiang from a family of Shanghai-based intellectuals, whose lengthy attack on Wu Han's *Dismissal of Hai Rui* was one of the very early triggers for the cultural struggle about to engulf the country. Yao makes clear in his polemic that there is no such thing as mere history. History is the story of class struggle. It comes laden with ideology and meaning. 'Since there were classes and states in human society, such a thing as "officials making decisions in favor of the people" has never occurred in the world,' Yao complains about the portrayal of Hai Rui as a simple, honest official working on behalf of the public.

> In China, neither the reformers of the landlord class nor the bourgeois democrats have ever brought 'good times' to the peasants. Only the great revolution led by the Chinese Communist Party – which has thoroughly smashed the state machinery of the landlord class and the bourgeoisie and founded the People's Republic of China led by the proletariat and based upon the worker–peasant alliance – has solved the problems of 'land, food, and clothing' for the peasants south of the lower reaches of the Yangtze River and the whole country. This is an ironclad fact which nobody can refute.[12]

Yao was to maintain his attack the following year through the literary, rather than the overtly political, launching of another sustained attack on, amongst others, the writer Deng Tuo (1912–66), resulting in the latter's suicide. Yao himself was felled almost as soon as Mao died, and incarcerated into the 1990s, before living largely in anonymity in Shanghai till his death.

Mao's conviction was that the burden of Chinese traditional culture was so heavy that only the deployment of violence would serve to shift it. Participants had to 'smash all the old conventions', he demanded to other leaders in 1966. 'The present great Cultural Revolution is a heaven-and-earth-shaking event.' It would lead to 'the final destruction of classes'.[13] The key work was to struggle, criticize, and then be transformed. 'Struggle means destruction, and transformation means establishing something new.'[14] Jiang Qing echoed this desire for profound transformation. 'We must popularize; popularization is our basis,' she declared to a group in the performing arts in Hangzhou in 1968. 'The fine arts must produce a few model works.'[15] It was extraordinary, she went on, 'that here in Zhejiang [the province Hangzhou is located in] [you] should be performing old plays and ghost plays to such an extent. You even have ossified corpses turning into ghosts and emerging from coffins.'[16] A middle school in Beijing produced a long list of prescriptions about the new culture being promoted in the late 1960s: 'Bookstores for classical books must this minute stop doing business.' They needed to 'clear away all poisonous weeds' so that 'these goods of bourgeois ideology' could never again be poured into the minds of the youth. Painting, sculpture, athletics, even amusement parks: they all needed to be reformed, changed – or simply abolished.[17]

Smashing old culture might be liberation, but it manifested itself in the violent act of destroying artefacts found in the houses of people who were under investigation as class enemies, and which were seen as being connected to the old world. Even sites as sacred as Qufu, the home of Confucius, were attacked. Temples and mosques were desecrated. Churches were turned into charnel houses or warehouses. Red Guards were only prevented from storming the Forbidden Palace in Beijing in August 1966 by the intervention of Premier Zhou Enlai, who instructed the Beijing Garrison to protect the museum, locking the entry doors. It was to remain closed till 1971.[18] The playing of Beethoven's music (nicknamed 'Old Bei' in Chinese) was forbidden, despite the great composer's deep links with revolution in his own time.[19]

'Who Hits Me, I Hit Back': Social Divisions

Even if there were people who gained from the experience of the CR, the costs of intra-elite fights in Beijing and the turbulence in society meant that this particular phase of China's march to renewal and regeneration was a fraught one. Of all the aspects of the CR, it is the way in which it exposed deep fissures across Chinese society, both in cities and in the countryside, and gave space for the expression of resentments, that is amongst the most disturbing. As Yang Jisheng did with the history of the famines, so journalists, scholars, and others, inside and outside China, over recent decades have painstakingly pieced together not just the political but also the social history of this era.

Subsequently, claims of extraordinary levels of violence within society have emerged throughout the whole of China, in some of the most isolated and remote areas. Novelist Zheng Yi's account was one of the earliest, and amongst the most shocking, detailing stories of cannibalism in Guangxi in the south-west over 1968. 'On July 10, 1968,' one witness tells him, 'a criticism rally was held in front of the Shangjiang town hall, Sanli District. During the ensuing chaos, Liao Tianlong, Liao Jinfu, Zhong Zhengquan, and Zhong Shaoting were beaten to death. Their bodies were stripped of flesh, which was taken back to the front of the brigade office to be boiled in two big pots.'[20] Twenty people were accused of subsequently devouring the meat. Unfortunately, Zheng's testimony is far from isolated.

As shown by Ralph Thaxton's work on the Great Leap Forward and the famine eras, referred to in the previous chapter, there were plenty of grounds for resentment and simmering desire for revenge in society, particularly against officials or those in local power networks who were believed to have exploited others. The general breakdown of order in the CR meant that those who wished to had plenty of opportunity to enforce vigilante justice, or take action on jealousies, prejudices, and a feeling that they could now rectify past injustices. Scholar Yang Su has documented the extent of collective killings in rural

China through the CR period – and shown that these were largely not the result of any state support, but occurred spontaneously, in different regions and for different reasons.[21]

Amongst the most powerful such testimony to the way the CR reached deep into the countryside, and affected even the most un-elite of places, can be found in the reports of journalist Tan Hecheng. He writes hauntingly of his wandering through an eerily quiet Daoxian county in Henan during the summer of 1966, only to find, decades later, that around this time the area was consumed by bloody massacres between different groups and individuals. Zhang Ming'ai, one of the protagonists, decided to deal with a neighbour by nailing his hands and feet to a wall and butchering him with the ancient 'death by a thousand cuts' method. His victim begging for mercy had no impact on him. 'Should I have mercy on you and wait for you to come and kill me?' he is reported as saying, 'This is a fight to the death – it's you or me.' With that, he dismembered his victim.[22]

The ubiquity of violence across the country, with no easy explanation for it (this was not a time of war, either civil or international), is one of the aspects of the CR that continues to be of concern. The semi-insurrection in the central city of Wuhan in July 1967 (the so-called 'Wuhan Incident') can at least be explained by a political narrative: the clash of factions attempting to claim allegiance to Mao and enforce their own revolutionary vision. The severity of this, along with other incidences over the coming months, was sufficient for Mao to call in the one institution which seemed capable of restoring order and remaining wholly loyal to him: the PLA, under the leadership of the man who would be his chosen successor before his own downfall in 1971, Lin Biao (1907–71). The ideology and practice of class struggle which lay at the heart of the CR in Mao's mind was unlikely to bond people together, even were there no other cultural or historical causes to create conflict between them. The theories of family background, and of 'birth' legacy, where people were consigned to a particular class almost like India's traditional caste system, with a treatment and fate associated with that class, was divisive enough, as the explanations of it by Chinese historians Yan Jiaqi and Gao Yuan have shown.[23] But this alone can hardly explain the sheer intensity, diversity, and virulence of the violence that swept across China over this period, and percolated through not only political and social elites, but other areas of society too.

For participants like the writer Ba Jin (1904–2005), this question of culpability was never to be dispelled. Writing in the more liberal era after the CR, in the 1980s, he admitted that despite being one of the victims of that period (together with his wife), 'the responsibility for all of this does not lie solely with Lin [Biao] and the Gang [of Four]: They could not have managed it by themselves, and it is high time that we all faced the truth of our own complicity; they could not have done it if we had not let ourselves be taken in.'[24] For someone of Ba's background, the CR was truly a holocaust, albeit a spiritual rather than a physical one. It was a movement that held up brutally to Chinese people, to this day, something about the vulnerabilities and the fault lines of their own society. Perhaps this is why attempts at a general assessment of the meaning of the era, beyond that contained in the 1981 CPC Resolution on history referred to in the previous chapter, which labels it simply a great mistake before moving on, have never been properly attempted in China to this day.

The Mystery of Lin Biao

By 1969, with a semblance of order restored through imposition of what was in effect martial law, a Congress, the first since 1958, could be held. The Ninth Party Congress in Beijing that April must have been a surreal affair. Photos in the official *Red Flag* magazine showed slightly bewildered delegates appearing to vote for the new leadership. They had good reason to look apprehensive. Of the 279 who were eventually elected onto the Party Central Committee, only fifty-three had been in the previous one.[25] Others had been imprisoned, or suffered worse fates. The historical significance of the event was to mark the brief, but important, period during which Lin Biao figured as Mao's chosen successor. Lin was one of the great marshals during the Communist victory over the Nationalists in the Civil War. He had, however, lived a somewhat shadowy existence in the decades since. Testimony after his death referred to his reclusive behaviour, along with claims (which are standard in Chinese-style attacks from this period) of being no more than a puppet for his very forceful wife, Ye Qun. Rumours of his poor health had been in circulation even during the period when he was most in the public eye.[26] Lin had been a faithful proponent of Chinese autonomy and self-resilience, in works like his speech observing the twentieth anniversary of the victory in the Second World War, 'Long Live the Victory of the People's War', delivered in 1965. By 1966, he had become amongst the most zealous of believers in the new movement, appearing alongside Mao at rallies in Tiananmen Square in central Beijing. He was the deviser of the *Quotations from Chairman Mao* (famously called the 'Little Red Book' because of its plastic cover), which had originally been issued to soldiers to help unify their thinking. This was to be printed to such an extent for wider use that it ranked as the most copied book in the world by the 1970s. 'The present situation of the great proletarian cultural revolution is excellent,' Lin stated at a rally in November 1966. 'The gigantic, vigorous mass movement is developing in depth with each passing day. A tremendous change has taken place over the whole of society.'[27] This was not so much a report on progress towards the desired utopia waiting for China as a declaration that it had already arrived. At the 1969 Congress, taking place against a backdrop of deteriorating relations with the USSR which ended in fierce skirmishes on the north-eastern border, Lin managed to have himself named as Mao's chosen successor in the Party Constitution.[28] The same constitution also restored explicit mention of Mao Zedong Thought as ranking alongside Marxism-Leninism as the guiding ideology of the Party, something that had not been the case since the Yan'an period a quarter of a century before.[29]

Lin Biao's ascent was to prove short-lived. In a confusing series of events in 1971 he departed from China on a plane heading towards Moscow. This crashed in the Mongolian People's Republic, killing him, his wife, and his son. Claims in material produced in China after his death stated that he had been planning an assassination of Mao and a coup d'état in the period before his flight. It is not even clear that his departure was voluntary, or that he was destined for Moscow. Lin has never been rehabilitated in China, and no consensus has been reached about what precisely did cause him to flee. His death, however, marked a new phase for the CR. It became less turbulent, and surviving leaders like Deng Xiaoping who had previously been sidelined were eventually allowed to return to central positions.

This did not stop the perpetual campaigns within the Party, which, while aimed at Lin once his claimed treachery had been exposed, were more intended to expose the living than the dead. The informal grouping of the Gang of Four, as they were subsequently labelled, were the main champions of leftism. They included Jiang Qing, Yao Wenyuan, Zhang Chunqiao, and the younger Wang Hongwen (1935–92), who had come to prominence as an activist in factories in Shanghai and who at the Tenth Party Congress in 1973 was elevated to the central Party leadership, gaining him the nickname 'the helicopter' because of this fast ascent. The Gang of Four, despite their prominence, had weak patronage networks – probably something that Mao intended. They existed at his behest, and they were to disappear almost the moment he died, all of them detained and then sentenced in the late 1970s. The 'Criticize Lin Biao, Criticize Confucius' campaign from 1973 was one of their main projects over this era, a strange combination of addressing the issue of cultural renewal by shredding what was claimed to be Confucius's malevolent influence over society, while also using the more contemporary reference to Lin to aim their attack at Zhou Enlai, the long-suffering but potentially more economically liberal premier. Zhou himself, assisted with the partly rehabilitated Deng Xiaoping, was to start promoting the notion of the Four Modernizations again. 'The reactionary programme of Lin Biao and Second Brother Kong [a reference to Confucius, whose Chinese name is Kong Zi] of "restraining oneself and returning to the rites" has already dealt a telling blow by the whole party,' one Big Character Poster of 1974 declared.[30] 'The criticism of Lin Biao and Confucius should be linked to the actual struggle in our city of Peking between the two lines,' stated another.[31] But the parallels were strained ones, and most invective was reserved explicitly for Lin, and implicitly for Zhou. Confucius figured just as an excuse.

Revolution on the Outside: Détente with the United States

Not the least of the many paradoxes of the PRC during the era of high Maoism – idealism and utopianism sitting beside horrific cruelty and inhumanity, anarchy alongside immense well-organized mass rallies and campaigns that took huge amounts of voluntary effort – was the way in which China's deep isolation also prompted its boldest diplomatic move: détente towards the United States.

China's relations with America had been in deep freeze since the Korean War. As its key alliance with the USSR fell apart, however, it began to seek more diverse partnerships. The troubles with Moscow were not ones that Mao took lightly, ordering a progressive move of key industrial and economic assets like aircraft factories and weapon-making facilities to the vast hinterland. This 'Third Front' policy explains why to this day China's aviation industry is split between huge centres in Xian, Chengdu, Harbin, and Shenyang, covering the length and breadth of the country. Mao himself in his idiosyncratic way ordered the Chinese to prepare for a likely attack by 'digging tunnels deep and storing grain everywhere', a slogan placed across the country on huge boards and repeated to bewildered US National Security Advisor Henry Kissinger in the early 1970s.

This conviction that the USSR was planning a full-scale imminent attack on China intensified as a result of the 1969 skirmishes between the two referred to above. It seems that around this time, Mao made the decision to mandate a small group of military figures then incarcerated in a prison in north-east China to brainstorm about whether, and how, to reach out to the United States. While berating the Americans as arch imperialists and 'paper tigers', strong in words and weak in action, and criticizing their role in the Vietnamese War then raging, at the same time private, more friendly messages were sent. One, too subtle for Richard Nixon's administration, was most certainly missed: the presence of American Edgar Snow on the rostrum for the October Day parade in 1970, a signal to the United States that China was reaching out to them. Back-channel talks were held, first in Poland, where the United States and China had representation, and then in New York, when China finally had its seat at the United Nations after a vote of members, replacing the Republic of China in 1971. Huang Hua, one of the most experienced of Chinese diplomats, and a figure who had survived the ravages of the CR largely by being posted abroad, in Egypt and then to the United Nations, was mandated to have deeper exploratory discussions. These culminated in a secret side-visit to Beijing by Kissinger in late 1971 while in Pakistan. Claiming stomach problems, he took a flight to the Chinese capital and held talks with Zhou Enlai, and eventually Mao himself, preparing for one of the great surprises of modern international affairs: a visit by US President Nixon himself to Beijing in September the following year.

Nixon's visit, his meetings with Zhou, Mao, and other figures (including a stern-looking Jiang Qing, with whom he attended one of the revolutionary operas), has acquired an almost mythical status now. It reshaped the global order. Mao and the sense of power emanating from him deeply impressed the US President. So too did witnessing Zhou Enlai redo the front page of the *People's Daily*, something Nixon wryly commented to his entourage he wished he had been able to do to the *Washington Post*, then pursuing him over the Watergate break-in. The agreement with the United States, for Mao at least, achieved the desired effect in sobering up the Russians. It was to irrevocably link the two former foes in ways which are still unfolding nearly half a century later. Nixon's calculation was a pragmatic one, however, something he had acknowledged even before becoming President when he stated in an article in *Foreign Affairs* that, despite his long record as an anti-Communist, no one could deny a fifth of humanity their proper diplomatic space.

Mao had declared during the final years of his life to a number of visiting dignitaries that the CR was, alongside the victory over Japan and unifying the country, likely to be his most enduring achievement. But even during his lifetime, weariness with the movement and its utopianism and impracticality spread. Deng Xiaoping had been one of the many who had noticed that for all the rhetoric of Maoism, something was amiss. While working in Jiangxi at a tractor factory in 1971, according to his biographer Ezra Vogel, he had noticed the poverty around him. His daughter Deng Rong, who was able to visit him, told him of how in rural areas in Shaanxi she had visited families who lacked toilets and pig pens. 'All of the children reported to their parents that the peasants did not have enough to eat or wear.' Absorbing this, Deng, by the time he left Jiangxi, 'had no illusions about the seriousness of China's problems and about the depth of change that was needed'.[32] The simple fact is that over two decades of revolution had not produced the economic and developmental aspirations that had originally been promised. As historian John King Fairbank commented, 'By the time Mao died,' on 9 September 1976, 'his revolution was dead too.'[33]

5

Reform and Opening Up
(1976–1989)

During his now almost legendary tour of the southern part of China in the era of instability a couple of
years after the Tiananmen Massacre of 1989, paramount leader of the time Deng Xiaoping reportedly
declared that 'without reform, there is only one road
– to perdition'.[1] The reference to the idea of two paths
echoed an earlier Maoist mantra: the struggle of the
two lines, capitalism and communism. Even in the
1960s, Deng was admired by the Chairman for his
immense competence, but also slightly distrusted
for what was perhaps regarded as a lack of commitment to the Maoist cause. That he had survived the
CR was a remarkable testament to the value that Mao
placed on his administrative abilities. On Mao's death
in 1976, Deng's re-emergence figures in many of the
subsequent accounts almost as though it had an air
of inevitability about it. At the time, however, Deng's
pragmatism and his involvement with earlier itera-
tions of the 'Four Modernizations' – things which are
presented now as his great strengths – were seen as
huge black marks against his name.

At the time of Mao's death the assumption by many
observers was that the radical leadership around him
given the label 'Gang of Four' were likely to prevail –

or at least their policies were. In 1975, one of the leading members, Zhang Chunqiao, had written a fiery text, 'On Exercising All-Round Dictatorship over the Bourgeoisie': 'There are new weeds engendered by the old soil of capitalism,' he wrote. 'At no time should we forget this historical experience in which "the satellites went up to the sky while the red flag fell to the ground", especially when we are determined to build a powerful country.'[2] State ownership was the correct path to this grand aim of building this great country – or rebuilding it. That meant no foreign capital, no markets, no entrepreneurialism. 'The "bourgeois" wind blowing from among those communists, particularly leading cadres, who belong to these "parts",' Zhang warned darkly, 'does the greatest harm'. These individuals 'poison', 'do harm', 'scramble for fame', and 'feel proud instead of ashamed'.[3] Deng was not explicitly referred to in this attack, but it was clear that he belonged to what Zhang and his allies figured was the devil's side.

With rhetoric like this it is easy to see why so few observers, even inside China, foresaw the changes that were about to happen once Mao had gone. The protests during the 'sweeping of the tombs' Qing Ming festival in April 1976, when people openly mourned the death of Zhou Enlai a few months earlier, and seemed to be making an oblique criticism of the current leaders; the clumsy handling in July of the massive earthquake in Tangshan, in the north, which saw over a quarter of a million people perish, when the Chinese government insisted on receiving no help from the outside world to demonstrate its autonomy; the sense of malaise and political apathy around Mao: these were all only properly seen as signs of deep problems portending imminent change later. As documented by Roger Irvine in a book on forecasting China's trajectory, in 1976 'few international observers foresaw the likelihood of China's emergence in the future as a stable and prosperous country'.[4] One of the very few who did have the foresight to see these changes was Stephen Fitzgerald, an Australian scholar and at the time Ambassador to China. In declassified cables he wondered why people did not think China could follow Japan's track since the war and raise its GDP and industrial output sharply. Even more prophetically, he foresaw by 2000 'the extension of dominant Chinese power and influence through the region'.[5] The Maoist objective had been to regenerate and renew China. It had at least unified the country, and built some infrastructure. The main challenge now was to see a change of tactics to try to achieve the goal that Maoism had attempted, but so far failed to reach. Deng's pragmatism, and his huge prestige in the Party as a member since the 1920s, a veteran of the war, and someone who was largely unencumbered by involvement in the disaster of the CR, stood him in good stead.

Ideological Battles in the 1970s: The Three Paths

If the narrative of Deng's inevitable re-emergence is something that can be contested, so too can the idea that once he had gained prominence, his 'opening up' philosophy was received with complete alacrity and uniform enthusiasm. The official government story today is of a pleasing transition between the madness of the 'turbulent decade' (as the CR is now called, if it is ever referred to in official Chinese government discourse) and the prosperity and continuous success of the Deng era. Scholars like Frederick Teiwes and Warren Sun, amongst others, have shown, however, that this is far too straightforward. Deng certainly did not work alone when he was restored to a position of responsibility after his previous removal from power in early 1976 during the Maoist period. Hua Guofeng (1921–2008) had been Mao's final choice of successor, a former leader in his native Hunan who had been brought to Beijing at his behest in 1971, and appointed head of the Party a month after the Chairman's death in 1976. According to Teiwes and Sun, despite the personal political struggle that did emerge between the two potential successors, 'On all key dimensions – the overambitious drive for growth, a newly expansive policy of openness to the outside world, and limited steps to management reform – Hua and Deng were in basic agreement.'[6]

Of the various options open to China in the late 1970s, the vision which was to prevail was that without a strong material basis China's grand march towards modernity would not be successful, and that the best means of attaining this was through purely economic means. In an oblique way, Deng was the mouthpiece of this message in the hugely important Third Plenum of the Eleventh Party Congress in December 1978. Held in the Jinjiang, a military hotel in Beijing off-limits even to this day to observers, the meeting was on the surface a standard Party affair, with stodgy speeches and cadres attending dressed in revolutionary-era uniform. While dense with references to the importance of respecting and maintaining commitment to Mao Zedong Thought and upholding Maoist revolutionary lines, the communiqué issued after the meeting contained a great ideological shift in its acknowledgement of the importance of 'improving the livelihood of the people' on the basis of growth in production.[7] In lines exhaustively repeated since then, it was declared that 'practice is the sole criterion for testing truth' and that 'the whole Party and the people of the whole country [need to] emancipate their thinking and follow the correct ideological line'. In a gentle, but effective, sideswipe at the dogmatism of the previous decades, the communiqué declared 'for a party, a country, or a nation, if everything had to be done according to books, and thinking became ossified, progress would become impossible, life itself would stop and the Party and country would perish.'[8] The books were presumably those hefty tomes of Marx, Lenin, and Mao which had been quoted at every turn from the mid-1960s onwards, and which could now be gently restored to their place on the shelves. The final words of the communiqué were, however, wholly consistent with the ethos of the Maoist period:

a commitment 'to advance courageously to make a fundamental change in the backward state of our country so that it becomes a great, modern, socialist power'.[9] The dream at least had been maintained. But the communiqué, and the Congress on which it had been based, did the important work of clearing a space where it was permissible to experiment and test out ideas like the market (through the household responsibility system, rehabilitated from the 1960s), openness to foreign capital (the first US–China joint venture, a Coca-Cola bottling plant, was opened in Tianjin the following year), and entrepreneurialism (the foundation in the early 1980s of Town and Village Enterprises).

The commitment to economic change and reform had been made. It just needed working out in practice. But from 1978 over to 1979, those who had participated in the CR and who had been radicalized and politicized by its contentious atmosphere took part in the Democracy Wall campaign to support a stronger focus on the political not just the economic narrative. One of these was an electrician at Beijing Zoo, Wei Jingsheng (1950–). Like Deng, whose experience of poverty while labouring in Jiangxi in the early 1970s had caused him to make a fundamental reappraisal of his world-view, Wei was exposed while travelling in the remote north-western province of Gansu to a sight he could not comprehend in a socialist country. 'In a crowd of youngsters below my [train window],' he recalled later, 'I noticed a young woman, her face smeared with soot and her hair covering her upper body.' But he realised something even more distressing: 'I had seen something that I could never have imagined or believed before: Other than the long hair spread over her upper torso, that young woman of about seventeen or eighteen years of age had absolutely nothing covering her body.'[10] Wei went on, 'From then on, whenever I read glowing praise in the newspapers for the "superiority of socialism" or heard people brag about how socialism was better than capitalism, I would swear silently, "Bullshit".'[11] For Wei, talk of Four Modernizations was pointless without a fifth, in the political realm: democracy. It was not just a case of improving material wellbeing, and focusing on the economic alone: 'To achieve modernization,' Wei wrote in a Big Character Poster put up on the West Beijing Xidan district wall in early December 1978, 'the Chinese people must first put democracy into practice and modernize China's social system.'[12] While the authorities were initially tolerant of opinions like these, their patience was to vanish in the early part of 1979. The compact had been reached. Yes to economic reform, but no to anything that looked like it would create organized political opposition to the CPC. Wei was sentenced to fifteen years in jail for state subversion in 1979.[13] After a further trial in 1994 following a brief period of liberty and another hefty sentence, he was sent into exile to the United States, where he lives to this day.

Apart from those who wanted more democratic

reform, the Deng leadership had to reckon with leftists: those who had deep misgivings about any notion of moving away from Maoist purity, and were deeply opposed to any notion of the market, and of private enterprise. There were a variety of figures in this group. The radical leadership around the Gang of Four had been dealt with by putting the ringleaders on trial, and throwing them in prison. But there were many more at large who still subscribed to the old-style autarkic economic model used up to 1977. Some, like Chen Yun (1905–95), were to remain in influential positions on the Politburo into the 1980s, and were to defend the dominant role of central state control. Chen was to coin the famous phrase that the market in China existed like a bird in a cage. It needed parameters and boundaries. The state with its political authority supplying overall direction always had to be there. Others, like Deng Liqun (1915–2015), were even more purist, opposing moves to liberalize the state-owned enterprises and allow more foreign capital. Deng Xiaoping, after his final ascendancy in 1980, was able to accommodate these figures but had to do so in ways which at least placated some of their concerns.

For all the respect paid to Mao, at least on the level of rhetoric, finding some way of managing his legacy and ensuring that his often destructive, emotion-driven politics did not return was one of the key challenges of the Hua–Deng leadership. Wholly repudiating Mao meant finding answers for why exactly for long periods Deng, and in later years Hua, had worked so faithfully under him. It also risked antagonizing a huge audience fed a relentless diet of praise about Mao for most of their life. The oft-repeated formulation of '70 per cent correct, 30 per cent wrong' was not actually used in the document where these matters were finally – at least as far as the Party was concerned – laid to rest, the 1981 Resolution quoted in the previous chapter. But it made clear that while Mao was a great leader, and a great theorist, and while Mao Zedong Thought was one of the treasures of the Party's indigenous development in China, 'chief responsibility for the grave "left" error of the "Cultural Revolution", an error comprehensive in magnitude and protracted in duration, does indeed lie with Comrade Mao Zedong'.[14] Unlike in the process of de-Stalinization in the USSR, there would be no wholesale repudiation of Mao's unique status and role. Instead, he was to remain on a pedestal, respected, admired, and increasingly irrelevant.

The Means to Economic Transformation

With the strategic commitment to accepting that economic reform was permissible, and justifiable because it would lead to creating the material basis for Chinese national rejuvenation and renewal, a series of specific policy changes were made. In keeping with the mantra of making practice the sole criterion for truth, these were often based on innovations and experimentations at grassroots level, which, if they succeeded, would then be adopted more widely until they became national policy. In the 1980s, China became at times like a vast experimental zone. Yasheng Huang characterized the whole period up to 1989 as the entrepreneurial decade. Even more surprisingly, over this period 'private entrepreneurship was developing most vibrantly in the poorest and most agricultural regions of the country.'[15] One measure of this is the number of those classified as living in absolute poverty. This fell from 250 million in 1978 to 96 million a decade later.[16] Chinese leaders, largely citing the World Bank and other authorities, are fond of saying that their government has done more to alleviate poverty than any other in history. But it would be more accurate to say that the administration under Deng Xiaoping as paramount leader (a term crafted for him to recognize his immense importance, despite having no formal role beyond chair of the military commission after relinquishing his Vice-Premiership in 1982), with, from 1982, Hu Yaobang (1915–89) as Party Secretary, did the most. In the 1980s, Huang continues, 'Chinese peasants experienced the most rapid income gains in history.'[17] Access to capital was easier, regulations more relaxed, and the ancient template of centrifugal rule in China changed, often dramatically. 'Rapid marketization across the board ... constricted the room for central plans and mandatory targets' which had been the core practice of Maoist state planning, according to Jao Ho Chung.[18] Vertical leadership was replaced by a philosophy of co-ordination, and mandatory targets were increasingly supplanted by advisory ones. For many investment decisions, and areas of industrial planning, provinces came to run their own affairs – as long as they paid decent tax revenue to the centre. This often meant that in key sectors like aviation and the automotive industry, China had dozens of different local enterprises where consolidation might have been more sensible and effective, but which, for status reasons, provinces wanted to maintain.[19] The one thing the centre did maintain control over was power of appointment. As Chung noted: 'Although many changes were introduced to the cadre management system in the last thirty-some years, the appointment, transfer and dismissal of provincial officials are still firmly controlled by Beijing so far as the crucial positions are concerned.'[20]

Deng himself acknowledged the often spontaneous nature of this transformation, brought about by the adoption of a more pragmatic governing philosophy outlined in the previous section where experimentation was allowed to see what worked. Referring to Town and Village Enterprises (TVEs), hybrid public–private entities established to absorb surplus labour freed up by large efficiencies in the agricultural sector, Deng stated in 1987: 'In the rural reform our greatest success – and it is one we had no means anticipated – has been the emergence of a large number of enterprises run by villages and townships. They were like a new force that just came into being spontaneously.'[21]

Anhui was one of the places of most innovation, attributed with the creation of the above-mentioned household responsibility system, where farmers were allowed to sell surplus grain above a target to the state for a profit. As one study put it, 'The rise of private enterprise and capitalism in China was neither envisioned nor anticipated by its political elite.'[22] The secret of the reform process was not that there was a plan organizing and stipulating things, but that there was no plan getting in everyone's way and hindering them. Nor could there easily be one when it was clear the leadership around Deng, for all the outward veneer of unity, did not have a clear consensus about what direction they were going in, and so tended to watch and wait till things happened before opining.[23]

Crossing the River by Feeling the Stones

The main components of reform in the 1980s during the high tide of liberalism were relatively simple. What had been anathema in the Maoist era was the acceptance of markets, foreign capital, and entrepreneurialism. All of these were to be tolerated, and then encouraged, as the decade wore on.

The reforms in the countryside around the household responsibility system were to have perhaps the most profound impact. A country which had experienced mass famine within a generation was, by the mid-1980s, producing enough surpluses to feed itself comfortably and export agricultural produce. The enrichment of some areas and some individuals was to form the basis for a non-state sector and an entrepreneurial class that, by 2005, accounted for more than half of GDP growth. A more initially dramatic change, though, was to exploit the location of small towns like Shenzhen, Zhuhai, and the larger Xiamen, and their proximity to places like Hong Kong (still under British control), Macau (Portuguese), and Taiwan (*de facto* independent) which had ethnic Chinese populations, but were already wealthy, technologically and economically advanced, and therefore excellent places with which to create strategic partnerships.

The Special Economic Zones (SEZs), of which fourteen were set up in 1980–1, harked back, slightly, to the treaty ports and the special concessions within which foreign business was conducted in the colonial era prior to 1911. But this had been on terms unfavourable to China. The new SEZs were to fulfil a clear strategic purpose: using the one thing that China had plentiful supply of, cheap labour, in order to attract the things it needed, namely technology transfer and revenue through manufacturing for export. This was not a new idea. Japan, South Korea, Taiwan, and others had all deployed the same technique after the Second World War. China was simply to do this on a scale that no one else had ever tried before. Shenzhen is the most celebrated of the zones. An undeveloped area largely devoted to fishing and agriculture up to 1980 with a population of just under 60,000, it was fenced off from the rest of China, and devoted to attracting, in particular, Hong Kong business people who wanted to have larger factories and cheaper costs in order to make goods for export. Only in the late 1990s was Shenzhen allowed to make goods for the domestic market.

What the world was to see in the new economic zones, and in particular in Shenzhen, was the realization of 'letting practice be the sole criterion of truth'. Tower blocks and vast new industrial zones and residential areas appeared. The influx of a new class of people, migrant workers, recruited from outside in order to come to work in these immense new enterprises, meant the town almost in a matter of years became a city, growing to a million by the early 1990s, and then 6 million by the turn of the millennium.[24] In the 1980s, Shenzhen saw GDP growth rocket. In the middle part of the decade, for some years it rose to over 40 per cent. If anywhere exemplified capitalism with Chinese characteristics, this was the place. It was no surprise that this granted the SEZ a privileged status in the new history of the PRC. It came to embody the spirit of the revolution being undertaken. There were Red China sites, like that of the First Party Congress in Shanghai, or the Yan'an caves where Mao and his colleagues had been based in the 1930s. And then there were the hallowed spaces of the new China like the SEZs. In 2010, the then Premier Wen Jiabao (1942–) visited Shenzhen in order to reaffirm its symbolic importance in this Reform narrative: 'China's development and changes over the past 30 years have relied on reform and opening-up,' an official report of his tour noted, adding that 'the realization of the great rejuvenation of the Chinese nation will [continue to] rely on reforming and opening-up.'[25] A few years later in early December 2012, within weeks of being appointed Party Secretary, Xi Jinping was to also pay a visit – a feat he repeated in December 2018 to mark the fortieth anniversary of the 1978 changes. All of this reinforces the way that post-Deng leaders have desired to hitch themselves to the same successful 'reform with Chinese characteristics' formula he devised. To this day, one of the few large images of Deng which still exists in the country stares down from a hoarding over Shenzhen.

Results in terms of raw output of per capita and gross GDP spoke for themselves. In 1980, growth was an estimated 5 per cent, per capita GDP was US$202, and GDP US$202 billion. Within a decade the last two figures had almost doubled. Per capita GDP was US$341 and GDP was US$390 billion.[26] While the country's period of massive increases lay in the years after entry to the World Trade Organization (WTO) in 2001, it was the 1980s that laid the basis for this. China still lives, at least economically, in a period brought about by the Dengist reforms.

Making Money, Losing Faith

The Party may have made a commitment to a purely economic narrative, but that did not mean that issues of how to address social and political developments, particularly those that had arisen as a result of the changes in people's material well-being and wealth, vanished. The Party-state attempted to deal with this challenge by relentlessly keeping people focused on economics and practical, material matters. But the paradox of an ostensibly Marxist-Leninist Party adopting so many techniques of capitalism was not lost on many, inside and outside China. Deng was very aware of this. *Time* magazine quoted him in 1986 as saying: 'There are those who say we should not open our windows, because open windows let in flies and other insects. They want the windows to stay closed, so we all expire from lack of air. But we say, "Open the windows, breathe the fresh air and at the same time fight the flies and insects." '[27] By the mid-1980s, the formal label given to this danger of outside contamination was bourgeois liberalism and spiritual pollution. 'Spiritual pollution can be so damaging as to bring disaster upon the country and the people,' Deng said in October 1983. 'It encourages the spread of all kinds of individualism and causes people to doubt or even to reject socialism and the Party's leadership.'[28] While willing to countenance moves like asking elderly officials to retire and promoting younger ones, allowing more study abroad, and opening up parts of the country to the outside world, neither Deng nor his charismatic colleague who was head of the Party, Hu Yaobang, were willing to go further and countenance the Party losing its privileged space in society. As a small concession, from 1987, experiments in having multi-party elections at the village level were allowed. But villages did not formally belong to the five-level governance system recognized in the Constitution (which started at counties, one step up), and the limited diversity of candidates meant that political parties other than the Communists were not allowed to take part. People could stand as individuals, but not as representatives of anything else.

Clampdowns on intellectuals like the astrophysicist Fang Lizhi (1936–2012) and on dissidents remained a feature of the decade, as did purges within the Party against corruption and ideological lack of commitment. The former was linked to the new issue of Party officials now working more closely with business people, and having to deal with the wealth this group were enjoying while they stayed on relatively modest wages. The 1980s saw the emergences of new forms of expression through, for instance, the 'Scar Literature' phenomenon in the early part of the decade, where writers were able to give fictional guise to the sufferings of people during the CR period. But the parameters for this free space, which were always blurred at the best of times, were occasionally tightened up. Despite this, the savage treatment of intellectuals in the Maoist period did not reoccur. But there was nothing like the process of perestroika which was starting to figure in Soviet politics under the newly appointed leader Mikhail Gorbachev from 1985.

Crisis of faith is a strong term. But it accurately describes what the Party experienced in the era after the death of Mao. Maoism had been a living faith for many Chinese, touching the most intimate areas of their life. It had spoken to the emotions and idealism of many of them. The death of this faith left a population disorientated, almost recovering from an addiction. As historian Mark Elvin wrote,

> Chinese Communism did, during the time that it was a living faith [in the Maoist era] and not just a discredited shell, provide the Chinese people with a story by which to live. With its current disintegration [in the post-Mao era] they face the loss of not one [the traditional world-view prior to 1949] but two systems of belief and life-orientation within a single century.[29]

Rampant materialism and the marketplace were fine for some aspects of life. But the reforms that the CPC promoted were having far more complex outcomes and impacts. Religious observance, banned under Mao, was tolerated. Self-expression, after a period of conformity in terms of how people dressed and how they lived their lives, was back. Inequality started to reappear. 'In Mao's day we had more fairness,' a farmer is quoted as observing in a study by political scientist Ben Hillman of south-west China, 'but that's because we all had an equal share of nothing.'[30] Now there was something for people to clash with each other about. While the economic message of the Party was a hugely popular one in the 1980s, its ideology was increasingly remote.

Speaking at the Thirteenth Party Congress in 1987, the new CPC boss, Zhao Ziyang (1919–2005), had alluded to at least one way of attempting to address this crisis: by talking of socialism as one which existed in China 'with Chinese characteristics', making it more inclusive and appealing to local tastes. 'Building socialism in a big, backward Eastern country like China is something new in the history of the development of Marxism,' he stated.[31] China was doing something intrinsically *sui generis*. The need to preserve what it thought was its cultural integrity meant it had to innovate and change ideas from outside to suit its identity. But when Zhao addressed moves towards political reform, his list of proposals – separating Party and government; decentralizing powers; reforming the personnel system for cadres and the government structure; doing better at consulting with the public; and strengthening the socialist legal system – made clear the new concept he was outlining did not embrace multi-party systems. Even this programme was contentious for figures like Deng Liqun and the leftists now starting to coalesce around claims that Mao's legacy was being betrayed. But at least until 1989, comprehensive economic and some political reform was being contemplated.

Tiananmen Square: The End of the China Dream, Phase One

All of this was to shudder to a halt with the events of April to June 1989. Here Chinese internal and external issues came to a head. As Deng was to state when thanking troops who had been involved with the quelling of the unrest on 4 June, only two days after the Tiananmen Square Massacre, 'Dictated by both the international and the domestic climate in China, [the event] was destined to come.'[32] The visit by Gorbachev in May, the first by a leader of the USSR since the schism in the Maoist era, had been one of the issues which were blamed for precipitating the events of 4 June. The reforms he had promoted back home had captured the imagination of some in China, leading them to demand the same thing. More serious by far, despite finger pointing by the Chinese government, were the rising levels of anger against corruption and inflation.

The Tiananmen Square uprising was a moment of exposure for Chinese society, but also for the Chinese leadership. Differences between those broadly more liberal, and the leftists who wanted more state control and ownership, had been manageable during the years of transformation in the economic realm up to 1989. But over the middle part of the year, things started to spin out of control. There was also a generational issue. Deng and his fellow veterans had largely moved from the front line of politics. But through the

Central Advisory Commission, an informal gathering established in 1982, and chaired by Deng till 1987 (it was only finally disbanded in 1992), the elders still had immense influence over how policy was formulated and implemented. They were the ultimate 'backseat drivers'. And the crisis of June 1989 brought their views into direct conflict with those of figures from a younger generation like Zhao Ziyang.

The death of Hu Yaobang in April 1989, like that of Zhou Enlai thirteen years before, gave a pretext for early demonstrations. These escalated through May. This was not just a Beijing-centric phenomenon, nor one confined to students and intellectuals, but something that reached into urban industrial workers and other social groups. In Tibet protests connected to the death in January of the second most senior religious leader in the Buddhist hierarchy, the Panchen Lama, escalated. These reached a peak in March, before they were quelled by the local security services. The Party boss of the area at the time, Hu Jintao (1942–), was to subsequently go on to be country President and CPC head in 2002–3.[33] The Beijing unrest was initially based at the elite universities there, a hark back to the 1960s and the period of Red Guard activism at Tsinghua and Beida. But soon workers at factories began to show solidarity. This linkage between different classes, in the leadership's eyes, was ominous. They were facing the very united front they themselves had so often claimed to be representing. An ill-tempered encounter between Premier Li Peng (1928–2019) and the student group leaders, including Wuer Kaixi, a native of the Xinjiang region, was filmed on 18 May, and shown on live television. Li, wearing military fatigues, 'opened the meeting by saying that the Party and government were "concerned for the health of the fasting students [some students had started a hunger strike in protest the week before]"'.[34]

In papers released a decade after the unrest, the decisive influence that Party elders had on events as they unfolded was made crystal clear. While Zhao Ziyang tried to broker compromise, and was seen amongst the students close to tears in late May telling them he had come too late, it was the group with Deng at the centre who made the final calls. Humiliation when the Soviet Union leader came in May, along with larger protests in the sacred space of revolutionary Communist power, Tiananmen Square, meant that by early June figures who in their early careers had been used to the bloodiest acts of warfare decided to call in the troops. On 2 June the Politburo Standing Committee of the time (without Zhao, who had already been sidelined) met with Deng and other Party elders. Deng was categorical. The current turmoil was because of outside interference and agitation. 'The Western world, especially the United States, has thrown its entire propaganda machine into agitation work and has given a lot of encouragement and assistance to so-called democrats or opponents . . . people who are the scum of the Chinese nation.'[35] China needed two things to develop: 'A stable envi-

ronment at home and a peaceful environment abroad.'
The current situation was unacceptable:

> So long as history eventually proves the superiority
> of the Chinese socialist system, that's enough. We
> can't bother about the social systems of other coun-
> tries. Imagine for a moment what would happen if
> China falls into turmoil. If it happens now, it'd be
> far worse that the Cultural Revolution. . . . If the
> so-called democracy fighters were in power, they'd
> fight amongst themselves. Once civil war got started,
> blood would flow like a river, and where would
> human rights be then? . . . So China mustn't make
> a mess of itself. And this is not just to be responsible
> to ourselves, but to consider the whole world and all
> of humanity as well.[36]

After the meeting, the order was given. Because of
fears of sympathy for the protesters within parts of
the PLA, two crack regiments from outside Beijing
whose loyalty was undisputed were ordered to enter
the city in the early hours of 4 June and clear the
square. After announcements ordering the students
still demonstrating to leave, live ammunition was
used. To this day, there is no accurate account of how
many died. Estimates range from a few hundred into
the thousands.[37] In the ensuing weeks and months, a
clampdown meant that by the end of the year all those
accused of being ringleaders in the event, either in
Beijing or elsewhere, were in captivity or had fled the

country. One of the most eminent was the academic and astrophysicist Fang Lizhi, mentioned earlier, who first fled for refuge to the American Embassy, eventually being allowed to leave China in June the following year, initially to Britain, then to the United States.

Tiananmen Square, 1989, ended the aspirations within China to see political reform on a Western model. Most who remained either gave up their political aspirations or chose the hard path of being dissidents, committed to their struggle for the long haul. But the event also started to remove the more idealistic notions of people in the outside world who believed that through economic change China was on a trajectory towards becoming a multi-party democracy like those which existed in Europe or the United States. Deng had made the relationship between China and this world clear. It was to be one based on hard-nosed pragmatism. It eventually resulted in the CPC being more convinced that it was on the right path, and that it was justified in what it had done in 1989. It has never apologized for this.

6

Starting Over after Tiananmen (1989–2001)

Leadership succession had proved a perpetual challenge for the CPC. Mao's choices had been uniformly unsuccessful. Liu Shaoqi's slow move towards replacing the Chairman as the key decision-maker had ended with his removal from office and death in the CR. For Lin Biao, his few years of favour had finished in the wreckage of a plane somewhere in the remote Mongolian countryside in 1971. Hua Guofeng had at least survived, but was completely without influence and power after 1981, despite Mao's investing such huge faith in him before his death. Deng's choices had not been much better. Hu Yaobang had been sidelined in 1987, after concerted complaints by conservative elements in the Party. Zhao Ziyang was ousted because of the build-up to 4 June 1989, and lived the rest of his life till 2005 as a shadowy figure, under effective house arrest, occasionally glimpsed playing golf.[1]

The final choice of Party leader before the 1989 uprising, Jiang Zemin (1926–), was a surprise. 'The new leaders should do some things to show we will persist with reform and opening', Deng declared at a meeting on 27 May 1989 in Beijing. 'After long and careful comparison, the Shanghai Party Secretary, Comrade Jiang Zemin, does indeed seem a proper choice. I think he is up to the task.'[2] Jiang enjoyed the benefit of the doubt simply because others at the meeting did not know him. 'I don't know Jiang Zemin very well,' fellow veteran Wang Zhen (1908–93) said after Deng had spoken, 'but I trust Comrade Xiaoping to get it right.'[3] With that, Jiang was summoned to Beijing and appointed.

Jiang's background was in the automotive sector. A student at the Stalin Automobile Works in Moscow in the 1950s, he had returned to China later in that decade to work in Changchun in the north-eastern province of Jilin, the site of a major car factory, before transferring to Shanghai in the 1960s. In this city, he had risen to be mayor and Party Secretary by 1989, largely promoting Dengist reforms, but also able to deal with the unrest around 1989 without use of oppressive intervention or any loss of life. Jiang's public persona was a comical one: a figure who was proud of using his various foreign languages, from Russian to English to Romanian, in public, and not averse, as he showed during the state visit to the United Kingdom in 1999, to bursting out in song. This to some extent ameliorated the immense damage that had been done to China's international image because of 4 June by giving a slightly softer and more human image to its leaders. The period 1989 to 2001 came to be increasingly dominated by Jiang. He proved a surprisingly good choice, stabilizing the country after 1989, saving it from the worst excesses of the leftists, who were expecting reforms to be overturned in the economic realm, and then guiding the country through a series of challenges from democratization in Taiwan to entry to the WTO.

Aftermath of 1989: Steadying the Ship

To see the PLA turn its guns on students had been a huge shock to both foreign and Chinese witnesses. Academic Ding Zilin's son had perished that night. 'Since June 4th, the Chinese government has talked constantly about respecting its citizens' "right to exist",' she wrote afterwards. 'Yet five years ago guns and tanks deprived countless outstanding young Chinese men and women of their "right to exist" in a single night. This is nothing but hypocrisy.'[4] The PLA, after all, was the people's army. How, many wondered, had it become the murderer of the country's young, the very people it was meant to protect? The main consequence of the Tiananmen Square Massacre was that it stripped away the veneer of openness and liberalism that had seemed to exist till then, and undermined the whole narrative of the CPC being on the side of the public. Ruthlessly maintaining one-party rule trumped everything else.

For the outside world, the choice of how to respond to what had happened in China was a challenging one. Should pressure be piled on, or some other approach be chosen which was less extreme? Throughout Eastern Europe, there were signs that the grasp of Communism was weakening. In the USSR, there was a new reformist leadership, led by Gorbachev, a man British Prime Minister Margaret Thatcher said the West 'could do business with'. In the immediate aftermath of the 4 June Massacre, condemnation rained down on China from across the world. Images like that of the famous 'tank man', standing alone before the army proceeding along one of the vast boulevards in central Beijing and stopping them in their tracks, became one of the great icons used to attack Communism. But the George H. W. Bush administration in the United States was cautious, and did not completely isolate and ostracize China. Arguably, if there was a moment when it could have forced immense damage on the CPC, blocking its international space, and causing it economic pain, in order to see regime implosion and the creation of a new polity, this was it. But Bush, riding high in the opinion polls at the time, and able to make foreign policy largely autonomously, decided to be more moderate. 'He could,' historian Robert S. Ross argued, make 'unilateral compromises to salvage US–China co-operation.'[5] This was done because the interpretation in the White House of what was happening in Beijing was that there was an intense political struggle going on and that the United States had to do what it could to support the reformists.

On the face of it, Bush's calculation was vindicated. In 1991 into early 1992, Deng as ageing patriarch emerged from what was assumed to be retirement (he had relinquished his last formal position of power, Chair of the Central Military Commission, in 1989) to undertake a tour of the SEZs, now in existence for over a decade, in the south of the country. Because of its similarity to the imperial tours made by emperors in the past, and because of Deng's almost regal status, this event was subsequently labelled '*nanxun*': the term historians had come to use about such visitations in the Qing and before. For Deng, seeing the outcomes first-hand of what economic development had achieved was vindication enough. 'In the short span of the last dozen years,' he stated when on his tour,

> the rapid development of our country has delighted the people and attracted world attention. This suffices to prove the correctness of the line, principles and policies adopted since the Third Plenary Session of the Eleventh Central Committee [in 1978]. No one could change them, even if they wanted to. After all that's been said, I can sum up our position in one sentence: we shall keep to this line and these principles and policies.[6]

The evidence before Deng's own eyes as he looked over the industrialized Pearl River Delta led to one inescapable conclusion: 'We should be bolder than before in conducting reform and opening to the outside and have the courage to experiment. We must not act like women with bound feet. Once we are sure that something should be done, we should dare to experiment and break a new path.'[7] There was no reverse gear. Reform would continue, despite the upsets in the previous years.

The Party under Jiang and Deng had to keep an eye on another unwelcome development which sharpened their commitment to 'socialism with Chinese characteristics'. In late 1991, after seventy-four years in existence, the Soviet Union collapsed. The event sent shock waves across the world. For many in the West it indicated victory for capitalism and liberal democratic systems. The West had won the Cold War. In China, unsurprisingly, views were much more circumspect. Even before the events of 1991, specialists in Soviet Affairs in the country (and, after all, many Chinese had been trained in the USSR in the period up to the late 1950s, and therefore knew the Soviet system well, spoke and read good Russian, and had an emotional affinity for the USSR, despite the differences since) had detected signs of deterioration and malaise. 'The Chinese analyses of Soviet economic failings were a comprehensive indictment of its command economy and ideological dogmatism,' David Shambaugh has written.[8] There is a deep irony in this: in the early PRC era, with disastrous results, the Chinese Communists had adopted an even more centralist, even more ideologically dogmatic system than that followed by Moscow. But they were now surviving, even as the USSR, which had once been urging fundamental change on them, had been swept away.

Chinese analysts, ever since the demise of the USSR, have tried to understand what went wrong, and what lessons they might learn, from the events leading up to 1991. They concluded that the following factors were essential: to maintain unified Party leadership; to control the army rather than let it become a political entity in its own right; to prevent privatization overshadowing the state sector; and to resist ideological pluralism.[9] What every analyst in the PRC agreed as the years went on and events unfolded in the newly created Russian Federation was that Communism's collapse had led to economic and developmental regression, and that this model exemplified everything that they wished to avoid happening to themselves. While plenty of prophets of the 'End of History' thesis were marking time on China's ability to maintain its system, in a further twist it is likely that the Russian experience during the Boris Yeltsin era from 1991 to 2000 bolstered the position of the Party in Beijing. You might not like us, they could say to Chinese people, but then, pointing to the collapse of life expectancy levels and general destitution across Russia as it attempted to implement market reforms often urged on it by the West, look what you get if you decide to change and listen too much to others.

The Taiwan Strait Issue

The existence of two parallel Chinas since 1949 has always been a source of confusion and contention. When Chiang Kai-shek took refuge on the island of Taiwan with 2 million troops and followers, he carried with him the name and claims of the Republic of China, founded in 1911. To this day, Taiwanese years are counted from the fall of the Qing, with 2019 being year 107. Formally, too, the government in Taipei maintains claims on Mongolia, long after the PRC relinquished any and formalized its borders. Chiang created a government in a place with a complex relationship with the Mainland: one that had not figured in Imperial China except as somewhere where there had been some migration, and which had been under Dutch and then Spanish rule in the seventeenth century, before the creation of a brief dynasty by Koxinga (Zheng Chonggeng, 1624–62) seeking refuge from the Manchu takeover in the 1640s. Throughout the next two centuries, Formosa island, as it was then named, and the group of small islands around it, existed on the periphery of the Chinese world: a place where aboriginal peoples lived alongside Han settlers, many of them Hakka (a sub-group within the Han famous for their widely dispersed existence). Only in the very latest years of the Qing was Taiwan granted the status of a provincial entity. But it was ceded to the Japanese in the Treaty of Shimonoseki after Qing defeat in the Sino-Japanese war of 1895. Unified as part of the Republic of China when Japan was defeated in 1945, within four years it was once more autonomous, even if not independent, because of Chiang's insistence that his was the true government of Greater China, not that of the 'Communist bandits', as he dismissively called them. Taiwan engaged in a remarkable economic transformation over the 1960s and into the 1970s, using this as its chief route to survival even as it lost its seat at the United Nations in 1971, and formal diplomatic recognition from the United States eight years later.

Taiwan's most impressive achievement, however, was the largely peaceful transition to democracy. Chiang's death, a year before Mao's, in 1975 meant power passed mostly to his son Chiang Ching-kuo (1910–88). The younger Chiang, despite years under his father's influence, clearly had a different mindset. Repression of demonstrators supporting democracy and political reform in the Kaohsiung area at the south of the island in 1979 seemed to prefigure the kind of violent struggles for change that were then going on in South Korea. But through the 1980s, Chiang mandated a series of reforms which granted more space to groups that wanted to organize. Unions, media, and finally a new political party, the Democratic Progressive Party, were able to contest for power with the Nationalists, dominant till then. This culminated in 1996, with the first universal franchise elections for President.

Taiwanese society was complex. The native population, who had a history on the island going back over five thousand years, existed alongside migrants who considered themselves of Han heritage, but Taiwanese in nationality – some of whom could claim descent from people who had come to the island hundreds of years before. These existed alongside the 'new people':

those who had arrived from 1947 as the Nationalists fought, and lost, the Civil War on the Mainland. For this group, emotional bonds across the Taiwan Strait were strong. They mostly had a different identity. In *Taipei People*, his celebrated set of short stories, the author Pai Hsien-yung writes of the ways this group of people balanced their memories of life in another place with their existence in a new environment.[10] There was a hope for this group at least that one day reunification would happen, even as younger people considered themselves increasingly Taiwanese rather than Chinese, despite their Chinese heritage.

Whatever the changes in feelings about identity in Taiwan, what remained consistent was the resolute determination of the leaders in Beijing from Mao onwards never to renounce their claims on the island, or to recognize its independence. Mao himself, after the great opportunity to reclaim the island in the early 1950s which had been scuppered by the distraction of the Korean War and commitment of forces there, spoke to Nixon of China being willing to wait. 'When I go to heaven to see God, I'll tell him it's better to have Taiwan under the care of the United States now,' he stated to a visitor in 1973. 'We can do without Taiwan for the time being, and let it come after 100 years. . . . Why is there need to be in such great haste? It is only . . . an island with a population of a dozen.'[11] Deng, too, had taken a longer view of the issue: 'Perhaps the next generation will be wiser than us,' he is quoted as saying about Taiwan in 1978.[12] This, though, was predicated on there being no radical change in the status quo.

Jiang Zemin had been bold enough to set out clear boundaries for the management of cross-Strait issues in a speech in January 1995, just as the Taiwanese election campaigning was underway. 'Taiwan is an integral part of China,' he stated, and its separation from the Mainland was due to 'national betrayal and humiliation'. This made clear why the island mattered. It was the key unresolved issue from China's bleak modern past of victimization. With Hong Kong due to be returned to Chinese rule in 1997 and Macau two years later, Taiwan was the last piece of unfinished business: a critical part in the great jigsaw puzzle of the country's renaissance and resurrection to becoming a renewed, powerful, rich nation, and one that was finally unified.[13]

Jiang's framework for reunification, and the use of threatening military exercises by the PLA just off the coast of the island, had the net result of delivering a handsome majority to the Nationalist candidate, Taiwanese native Lee Teng-hui (1923–). The same gambit four years later had an even more disastrous outcome for the Mainland: the election of the Democratic Progressive Party candidate, and a strong supporter of greater Taiwanese autonomy, Chen Shui-bian (1950–). Cross-Strait relations entered an era of instability from which, despite occasional moments of stability, they have never really emerged since.

The New Narrative: Patriotism and Love of the Chinese Motherland

The muscular attitude towards Taiwan as it became an authentic democracy was partly fired by changes within the CPC after the Tiananmen Square tragedy and the collapse of the USSR. Isolated owing to its political system, and yet still economically prospering, China as a country, and the Party as a political force, were needing to find new sources of legitimacy. Class struggle and the Maoist aim for utopia had long gone. Delivery of a better standard of living and material outcomes had been successful since 1978, but with the crisis of faith in the Party's ideology referred to in the previous chapter and the growing chasm between its belief system and that of the wider society, the security of its hold not just on people's bodies, but also on their souls, seemed to grow progressively weaker.

One immense resource the Party propagandists could resort to in order to address this was that of utilizing the feelings of national pride which were being generated by China's economic success. This exploited a particular narrative of history supplemented by events like the return of Hong Kong, and by reinforcing the idea that the outside world was hostile to the country and that it needed to be unified under one-party rule to counter this.

Hong Kong's return figures large in this emerging nationalist narrative as the basis of Party legitimacy from the late 1980s into the 1990s. China under Jiang reaped an unexpected dividend over the city's reversion to Chinese sovereignty, which went far beyond the return of some very expensive, commercially successful property and a booming economy. It was able to use the drama of the negotiations with the British to prove that Communism – and particularly socialism with Chinese characteristics – worked in terms of making for more equal relations with the outside world. Restoration of sovereignty tangibly restored pride to China, and healed the wounds left from the history of national humiliation. From 1984, the British and Chinese governments had been working in earnest to create out of Deng Xiaoping's idea of 'One Country, Two Systems' (originally devised for the management of the Taiwan issue) a framework that would preserve the unique capitalist system in the city, but also allow for Chinese control. Hong Kong, after all, had manifestly shown that success was the criterion for truth as it built a world-recognized financial system. 'Within the PRC,' Deng stated to a visiting delegation from Hong Kong in 1984, 'the Mainland with its one billion people will maintain the socialist system, while Hongkong [*sic*] and Taiwan continue under the capitalist system.' He continued, 'Our policy towards Hongkong will remain unchanged for a long time to come.' There was no question of the city, as then British Prime Minister Margaret Thatcher had apparently hoped, continuing under British rule with an extended lease. Hong Kong was part of a history that now needed to be brought to a close. 'For more than a century since the Opium War, the Chinese people were looked down upon and insulted by foreigners. But China's image has been transformed since the founding of the People's Republic,' Deng stated. 'The Chinese and Hong Kong share this sense of national pride.'[14]

The Sino-British Joint Declaration of 1984 envisaged Hong Kong having a high degree of autonomy in every area except defence and international affairs. 'The current social and economic systems in Hong Kong will remain unchanged, and so will the life-style,' it promised.[15] This would continue for fifty years after 1997. The Basic Law agreed by the National People's Congress, China's parliament, passed into law in 1990, was to act as the city's *de facto* constitution from July 1997 when reversion to Beijing had occurred. This enshrined the various rights. But through the 1990s, there had been turbulence, particularly after 1992 under the last governor, UK politician Chris Patten. His focus was on delivering more democracy to the city through legislative electoral reform – something fiercely resisted by Beijing. While the handover in 1997 went ahead, it did so in an atmosphere tinged with feelings of mutual betrayal.

Under Jiang, patriotic education campaigns had been waged, at schools and then in society more widely. Those, like the author, living in China in the mid-1990s saw slogans daubed on walls even in the most remote parts of the country declaring the need

to 'love the country' and advertising the merits of patriotism. The spat with Taiwan in 1995 into 1996 had
been accompanied by an almost ceaseless diet of television and media coverage saying that Chinese people
would never again endure being humiliated at the
hands of outsiders.

The Zhu Rongji Reforms

The key task, however, for all the drama from Hong
Kong and Taiwan, remained to ensure that the Deng
legacy was maintained, and that reform and opening up continued within the framework of 'socialism
with Chinese characteristics'. Despite the impetus
given by Deng's Southern Tour in 1992, there could
be no complacency about continuing to implement
growth-supporting changes in the economic model.
Deng's death in 1997 occurred several years after he
had largely become politically inactive (his last public
appearances had been in 1994, as a frail nonagenar-
ian). The main thing was to claim his legacy, something that Jiang had to do against critical voices within
the Party itself. One of these, that of the ideologue
and high priest of leftism Deng Liqun, was probably
behind a 'ten-thousand character' manifesto that sur-
faced in 1996. This document criticized the rise of
private entrepreneurs, the poor calibre of cadres, their
distraction from governance and Party ideology by
doing business, and the general erosion on the socialist
state-managed system by market forces. 'Many people

mock the moral character of selflessness,' the letter complained. 'A worker from Shanghai said, "Alas, I have woken up. Diligence cannot lead to affluence. I must change my concepts, wipe out my past thinking, and try to engage in business."'[16] The culture of the Party had been mired in corruption, spiritually and materially. The lessons of 1989 had not been heeded. For this group, what had happened then was not because reform was too slow, and not making people better off, but precisely because reforms had brought about materialism, self-centredness, and the disintegration of the Party's moral authority.

This was a powerful critique, one that as good as labelled reformers traitors to their own Party. The liberals' rejoinder was mainly to demonstrate that continuously better material gains for as many people as possible was the whole point of socialism and always had been. But the strength of their argument was also its main vulnerability: that the CPC was using economic benefits to buy people's loyalty. New sets of reforms were constantly needed to generate growth to keep up with demands.

In the late 1990s, the main target for change was the state sector. Bloated and often deeply inefficient, employing far too many people, it was in desperate need of greater enterprise and innovation. The figure spearheading this was the much admired Zhu Rongji (1928–), Premier from 1998 to 2003, and a colleague of Jiang's who had come from Shanghai with him. He worked on a blueprint for kickstarting the Chinese economy to move it into the new phase of reform. Zhu was a veteran of the 1950s Anti-Rightist campaign, and was jailed and then disciplined over this period. A tough boss, he was the epitome of a hands-on manager, hugely admired not only by those in the CPC but also by the outside world. During one visit to the north-eastern Heilongjiang province, one official had displeased him so much he had fired him on the spot. Asked at another international meeting whether the media could talk to him, he had handed out his fax number. Zhu's high standing in the CPC meant he was able to announce dramatic changes in the state sector, addressing its deep-seated structural issues.

One of the most important of these was lack of meaningful competition. State ownership of huge work units meant that they had few incentives to produce better-quality goods, with more variety, satisfying customers. Constant guaranteed revenue meant that they had little reason to change. However, while state enterprises had not changed, the public had. Poor-quality goods were being sold to customers who were increasingly demanding, and expected, better service and standards. As foreign joint ventures came into China, their goods showed up the shoddy quality of their Chinese counterparts. How could the country achieve its great regeneration project if it remained dependent on this kind of foreign control and influence? The China dream had to include making companies like the Japanese and South Koreans had. That meant cutting the vast state enterprises down to size; getting rid of the notion that every province needed its own aviation, or automotive, works; and allowing market forces to decide what did, and did not, get made. Over the late 1990s, as consolidation amongst state enterprises proceeded, and central ministries were reduced in size, as many as 60 million lost their jobs. Accommodation and services that had once been handled by the old *'Danwei'* work unit system, with its mentality of the 'iron rice bowl' and cradle-to-grave provision of social welfare, were put out to non-state tender. People were able to buy their own homes, set up companies, and increasingly express their own economic agency.

Part of the Zhu plan had been a shrewd use of foreign investment and involvement to supply much-needed competition internally. In this way, state enterprises would be forced to innovate and change, or go to the wall. Originally as part of the General Agreement on Tariffs and Trade (GATT) from 1986, the PRC had been negotiating to enter what, from 1995, had become the WTO. The march to WTO entry had been a tortuous one, and was almost achieved when Zhu visited the United States in 1999, only to be met with a President Clinton distracted by the fallout of impeachment attempts in Congress, and therefore unwilling to expend any effort on trying to get a contentious issue like Chinese trade agreements approved. More opening up to the outside world, however, was crucial, and while WTO membership was not finally achieved till 2001 (see next chapter), symbolic moves like China's application to host the Olympics, unsuccessful on the first attempt in 1993, but then fruitful in 2000, were all part of a huge project of rehabilitation after the Tiananmen 1989 events.

Social and Political Change in the 1990s

Rapid economic changes and the disruption caused by reforms like those Premier Zhu promoted in the state-owned enterprise sector inevitably had social impacts. Through the 1990s, inequality grew across Chinese regions, and increased rapidly within socio-economic groups. According to the Gini co-efficient, where 0 means absolute equality in income distribution and 1 complete inequality, while at the start of the reforms in 1980 China had a measure nationally of just above 0.3, showing reasonable levels of equality, by 2000 this had grown to 0.45, the kind of disparities seen in Latin American countries.[17]

Capitalism as it came into China created winners and losers, good and bad outcomes, and significant opportunity costs. Those who worked in the factories in the SEZs were a case in point. Mainly from rural areas, although earning more than they could ever have imagined before, they often lived in conditions akin to servitude while working, with no union protection (except from the single government-mandated union, which offered next to no support) and very little welfare. Of this new cohort of 80 million, by 1999 (it was to triple over the next decade) their plight was often a pitiful one. 'The millions of peasants roaming the country desperately looking for work to earn a hand-to-mouth living make up an almost inexhaustible pool of human machines,' Australian academic Anita Chan wrote at the time. 'They can be worked to breaking point, and when they flee these dreadful factories, they are simply replaced by fresh, vulnerable batches of workers.'[18]

There were still some who had not forgotten the heady atmosphere of 1989, and maintained the faith that at some point the discontent which emanated from emerging groups like those Chan was referring to would lead to meaningful political change. One such group, in the city of Hangzhou in 1998, tried to register the China Democracy Party. They were dealt with quickly, with over twenty activists being imprisoned the following year for state subversion, including the ringleader, Wang Youcai. The Open Declaration of the party stated:

> All political power can come only from the public and can only be [used] in the service of the public; a government can only come into being according to the wishes of the public and [can only] act according to the wishes of the public; a government is the servant of the public and not the one which controls it.[19]

Such a direct challenge to the legitimacy of the Party was simply not tolerable, and veteran activists from the 1980s like Xu Wenli were rounded up merely because of association with the Hangzhou group. Even the intervention of President Clinton during a state visit the same year did little to help things.

The feeling of perennial insecurity and suspicion in Beijing was fuelled by the appearance of a threat from a wholly unexpected direction: a group practising Buddhist breathing and meditation exercises called Falun Gong. Founded by a former PLA soldier, Li Hongzhi (1951–), the group had become popular in rural areas. There were also rumours that practitioners existed at the upper levels of the government. In April 1999, a protest in Tianjin, a city near Beijing, about a critical article on the group in a local newspaper met with violence from riot police, leading to a second demonstration, by 100,000 people, in the capital a few days later. The Beijing event was particularly worrying for Jiang Zemin and his fellow leaders for a number of reasons: it had appeared almost from nowhere; the protest had successfully managed to surround the central government compound at Zhongnanhai, one that was heavy with symbolic meaning; and the group were reputed to have over 70 million members.

The Beijing protest was peacefully dispersed. Over the ensuing years, however, Falun Gong was to receive a sustained, and sometimes brutal, payback. The movement was banned in 1999. Those who continued to practise were, it is claimed, sometimes subjected to horrifying physical and mental torture and maltreatment.[20] Despite this, two decades later there are still underground followers and adherents and it has healthy followings abroad, particularly amongst ethnic Chinese communities. Throughout episodes like this one, the position of the Jiang government was to consistently maintain that it supported human rights, but only collective ones, because of the undeveloped nature of the country.

Painting the Capitalists Red

One group who did find their status dramatically improved were the business people who had sprung up in the non-state sector throughout the 1990s. The term for this was 'xia hai': leaping into the river, something that was done by officials, former state enterprise workers, and in fact anyone who wanted to take advantage of the new entrepreneurial opportunities that were coming along. The leftists reserved particular spleen for this group. 'Some private entrepreneurs,' railed the 'ten-thousand character' manifesto attributed to Deng Liqun (see above), 'or those in charge of collective enterprises who insist on taking the capitalist road are subsidizing the bourgeois liberals in running newspapers and magazines, and establishing their so-called nongovernmental research, consultative and intermediary organizations.'[21] This group constituted a new bourgeois class, who, once they matured, would 'completely destroy the Communist Party'.[22] But in fact the striking feature of the business people in China since 1989 was the ways in which they had been largely so politically obedient. Even in 1989, a figure like Wan Runnan from the Beijing-based Stone Corporation who had offered support to students demonstrating 'had been the exception, not the rule'.[23] Nevertheless, business people were not allowed to apply for Party membership through the 1990s, and they and their enterprises occupied an often grey area. Yasheng Huang characterized the situation as one where there was 'a political pecking order', with the state sector sitting on top, able to enjoy subsidies, cheap utilities and land, and a host of other preferential policies. 'Amongst all the constraints on the growth of private firms,' he wrote, 'the low political and legal statuses of private firms are most fundamental and most blatant.'[24]

Despite this, the 1980s into the 1990s saw a raft of companies founded which were to go on to have a massive impact on growth and innovation in the country. Telecoms provider Huawei was set up in 1987, Lenova (originally Legend computers) in 1984, Alibaba in 1999, and ZTE in 1985. As these companies grew, the role of private entrepreneurs also became more of an issue. Could they be permanently marginalized, posing the potential for a threat one day from dissatisfaction at having no effective voice, or was there some way they could be co-opted and brought within the Party?

Jiang's solution was the latter. From 1999, through a campaign with the unenlightening name the 'Three Represents', he talked of there being a triad of areas which the Party defended: development trends of advanced productive forces; the orientations of an advanced culture; and the fundamental interests of the overwhelming majority of the people of China.[25] The first of these was the most significant, because of its reference to the non-state sector, and to private business people who were producing rising levels of growth and employment opportunities. Jiang's speeches in 2000 meant that by the Party Congress of 2002, the one in which he formally retired as Party Secretary and handed over to Hu Jintao, the Party Constitution was changed to incorporate the 'Three Represents', and to accept that non-state business people were now permitted to join the Party. A huge number took the chance to do so. This meant that they had shifted from being amongst the most despised figures in society in the Maoist period (many of the older entrepreneurs had indeed spent time under 'thought reform' or even in jail in the 1950s and 1960s) to the newest, and amongst the most effective, foot soldiers in the campaign to regenerate and rebuild the country. In the coming decade, they would also be key in participating in one of the most explosive eras of growth ever experienced by a human society over such a short period.

7

The Hu Jintao Era
(2001–2012)

Despite an almost complete lack of charisma, Hu Jintao had attracted the attention of Deng Xiaoping, who reportedly figured him as a future leader with the commendation 'I think Comrade Hu Jintao is not bad' during the 1992 Fourteenth Party Congress[1] – a form of words that would rate as a put-down in any other context except that of elite Chinese politics! The succession from Jiang to Hu had, on the surface, been one of the smoothest since 1949. Despite this, Jiang was accused of conserving his influence by ensuring that in the Politburo around the new leader from 2002 were his own protégés – figures like Zeng Qinhong (1939–) – and by maintaining his position for a further two years as Chair of the powerful Central Military Commission, the body in charge of China's army, navy, and air force.

While Jiang had often been an extrovert, keen to burst into song and show off his numerous foreign languages, Hu was largely uncommunicative, almost scholarly in his demeanour, and silent on his own biography. He reportedly had a photographic memory, and zero small talk. He was in his element in listing large amounts of data and producing speeches memorable for their dense use of slogans and lack of any sign of an individual human voice. These characteristics didn't matter, however, because as Hu was to be in charge when the country's economy simply rocketed, he could let the figures do the talking. The data indeed truly speaks for itself. Between 2000 and 2011, GDP went from US$1.1 trillion to US$6.9 trillion, effectively more than quadrupling. Per capita GDP rose from US$945 to US$5,183, a fivefold rise. Growth each year averaged nearly 9 per cent. This was despite the impact of the global financial crisis in 2008. The Hu Jintao era is about three things: growth, growth, and growth.[2] At the heart of this was China's final entry to the WTO in late 2001.

The New Long March: China's Entry to the WTO

China had started its negotiations to enter the WTO before the organization even existed. Back in 1986, GATT, set up as part of a post-war multilateral arrangement, was the target of Chinese negotiation. Once this had transformed into the WTO in 1995, and despite the significant hiccough of the 1989 uprising, China resumed negotiations. The final deal was secured in 2001, when the 160-plus other members of the organization also reached agreement with the PRC and it formally entered the organization.

Assessments of the impact of WTO entry at the time, inside and outside the country, were often pessimistic. China's state enterprises, despite a number of years of concerted reforms to make them more efficient under Zhu Rongji (described in the previous chapter), were still regarded as uncompetitive and reliant on state subsidies. The Chinese agricultural sector, which constituted more than a quarter of GDP despite the massive and historically important shift to manufacturing since 1978, was seen as even more vulnerable to international competition. Questions were also raised about how viable it was to open the whole services and finance sector to outside, much more experienced competitors in a matter of a few years (the WTO stipulated five years for compliance in most of these sectors). China, the most cautious of players, had taken a huge gamble. Banking companies, and multinationals, anticipated that the elusive market – the one that Joe Studwell, a British consultant, characterized as the 'China Dream'[3] – would finally be cracked open.

The Hu era was one where the landmark of WTO entry therefore had one indisputable manifestation: it ushered in a period of rampant GDP growth. This was not just a statistical achievement. It is true that in the decade from 2001, despite the pessimistic forecasts, China became the world's largest exporter, and second largest importer, and by the middle of the decade the holder of the largest amount of foreign currency reserves. Producing these kinds of statistical achievements became a favourite for Hu and his colleagues whenever they spoke. They could use the example of personal car ownership (doubling from the middle to the end of the decade),[4] tourists going abroad (which rose fivefold from under 10 million by 2010),[5] and the amount of energy produced. Less popular figures were the downsides of this rapid development: the bulk of the world's most polluted cities, polluted water, and congested roads. One thing was certain. In the 2000s, China became the global capital of vast statistics.

This breakneck sense of change was something patently obvious in the material world too. Motorways ploughed their way across the country. Skyscrapers shot up, sometimes with a floor a day added, in cities from Shanghai to Shenzhen. A migrant population of over a quarter of a billion, according to the 2010 national census, were the great infantry of urbanization, moving into new cities, meaning that when the Hu era had ended, China was for the first time ever a place where more people lived outside of the countryside than in it.

Canadian Chinese novelist Chan Koonchang caught the often giddying feeling of this time well in his satirical work *The Fat Years*:

I'm not blindly praising China. I know China has many problems. But just think about this. There was the 2008 financial tsunami, when developed capitalist countries led by the United States, began to self-destruct. They only enjoyed a couple of years of slight recovering before they fell into stagflation in 2011. The new crisis spread right across the globe, leaving no nation untouched. And now there's no end in sight to this depression. Only China has been able to recover, surging forwards while the others are on the decline. With domestic demand filling in for the dried-up export market, and state capital replacing foreign investments, the current forecast is that this year will be the third successive year of more than 15 per cent growth. Not only has China changed the rules of the international economic game, we've also changed the nature of Western economics. Even more important, there has been no social upheaval; in fact, our society is even more harmonious now.[6]

Chan's vision is a fictional one, albeit rooted in a particular view of reality. His book describes a country overwhelmed by self-satisfaction and pride, where these feelings of contentment that flow from growing progressively more wealthy reach almost epidemic proportions. It is easy to forget that however accurate the portrayal of a China reeling from these feelings of richness and success is, in fact underneath there were plenty of deep challenges and problems. Despite Chan's statement, the truth was that, far from being a harmonious era, China under Hu was one of contention. And much of this was in the rural areas, where many felt left behind.

The Life of China's Peasants: China's Sorrow

Anhui-based journalists Chen Guidi and Wu Chuntao produced the most widely disseminated description of what life in Chinese villages was like as the country implemented its WTO responsibilities. Commentators from a slightly earlier period like Cao Jinqing in *China Along the Yellow River* from the late 1990s wrote about the conditions in a rural China shifting from its age-old habits of activity and social structures.[7] For Chen and Wu, rural China was a place of inequality, injustice, and marginalization. During the 1980s, largely pro-urban, pro-coastal reforms had left many in rural areas feeling worse off, even though the household responsibility system had revolutionized production output and TVEs fundamentally changed rural business. Village elections, made nationwide as a result of a 1998 law, had done something to try to improve governance at the most basic level for China's 800,000-plus villages. But after WTO entry, rural China was suffering once more.

At the heart of this was the issue of tax. After improvements in overall living standards because of reforms since 1978, rural China started to grow more prosperous. 'In the ten years between 1990 and 2000,' however, Chen and Wu state, 'the total of all taxes that the state had extracted from the peasants had increased from a factor of five, from over 8.7 billion yuan to over 46.5 billion.' This meant that the tax burden per head on the average rural dweller was six times that of someone in the cities. 'But over and above regular taxation, the peasants had to suffer further extortion for village reserves and fees for social services.'[8] This was on top of one of their great burdens: the generally poor quality of local officials at this level, and the fact that they were often assessed just on keeping situations stable no matter what they did to achieve this. If that meant use of heavy-handed repression, and sometimes thuggery, then so be it. Chen and Wu cite one example of this, but the story was one that could have been told across the rest of the country. According to surveys, while central leaders were relatively trusted, provincial leaders ranked behind them, with county or village leaders looked upon as lowest of all.[9] There was one specific reason for this: with powers to gather taxes and implement increasingly unpopular policies around family planning, they were there often to do the state's dirty work. This echoed the situation in the 1960s described by Ralph Thaxton and cited in Chapter 3.

There was another set of policies that local officials were also busy dealing with over the Hu era which gained them even more bad press. The fiscal system meant that while the central government raised taxes, provinces were often those that had to do the spending. They relied often on disbursements from Beijing. Their expenditure for education, social welfare, and health kept rising, even as their revenue from Beijing remained relatively stagnant. With limited powers to raise their own taxes, one area where they could be enterprising was in sale of land, converting it from agricultural to commercial use. In the boom years, land once used for vegetables or livestock was often requisitioned by the local government, and the current users were compensated, and relocated, before it was redeveloped. The manner in which this was done, the generally modest levels of recompense, and the natural human aversion to being summarily turfed out of places where families had lived for generations meant that the sight of villagers in pitched battle with formal and informal security agents was common. Some of these disputes became close to all-out local uprisings, with one in Wukan in southern China attracting international attention in 2011. In these situations, the local officials had three choices: negotiate with protesters, send in the People's Armed Police, or take even more drastic steps to impose order. Failing to do so meant the end of someone's career as an official. Beijing made it brutally clear it was only interested in hearing good news.

Hu Jintao and Wen Jiabao were not immune to the complaints and suffering of rural China. It was in fact to be the target of perhaps the most important policy change they made: the lifting of all taxes in 2007. This significantly reduced pressure on farmers. Attempts, however, to reform the household registration (*hukou*) system, one which divided the population into two broad categories, rural and urban, granting them very different rights, and often prejudicial against the former, proved far more challenging. Only in 2019, under Xi, were there more systematic attempts to do this. And these, at the time of writing, remain a work in progress, with uneven levels of reform across the country.

Contention in the Cities

Nor were the cities and urban areas havens of peace and harmony during this period. As Hu started to refer to the 'harmonious society' in the run-up to the important 2007 Seventeenth Party Congress, drawing on ideas from Confucius and other thinkers rehabilitated back into intellectual life after the period of Maoist banishment, so it was clear that fast-paced economic development was changing not just the face of China, but also its heart. The most visible and sometimes frighteningly dramatic manifestation of this was in protests. These ranged from those involving only a few people, to others with hundreds and sometimes thousands participating. In a speech to Party officials in 2009, Yu Jianrong, a highly regarded social scientist in Beijing, estimated that there were 90,000 such incidents in the previous year. He divided these into those involving protests over legal rights issues, those which were to vent fury because of official malfeasance and mistakes, and then more opportunistic demonstrations which were by marginal urban groups just causing trouble.[10] Expenditure on domestic security to tackle this rising new phenomenon also grew exponentially.

The causes of such discontent were various. One was simply the ways in which the internet was spreading, with the number of users rising from only a couple of million at the end of the previous decade to almost half a billion by 2010.[11] From early on in this development, the government devised a number of ways of trying to rein in the politically disruptive potential of the world wide web. These included labour-intensive censorship by administrators spread across the country, but also the construction, master-minded by academic Fang Binxing, of the infamous Great Firewall. Gradually over the Hu era, sites from Facebook to Twitter to Google were blocked – along with news sources, from the BBC to the *New York Times*. The role of the internet for activists during the Arab Spring of 2010 only reinforced the commitment by Chinese leaders to vigorously defend what they called their 'cyber sovereignty'. Even in these restrictive circumstances, mobiles, smartphones, and the internet did allow groups to talk to each other and link up, often playing a complex game of cat and mouse with the authorities.

A more basic cause was the steeply rising levels of inequality. There were many areas in which this was shown. Across various regions, differences deepened, with the coastal ones often leaping ahead, leaving inland places to lag behind. The expectations of some segments of Chinese society rose. They wanted better service from government and the healthcare system. For some groups, pension provision was a cause of concern, with very incomplete coverage across socio-economic groups. For others, it was resentment at a legal system which was overburdened through demands from a new generation of legally more aware citizens who were often frustrated at getting court judgments, and then finding them hard to implement. Those who exercised their right to petition the central government when they felt that local officials had not addressed their concerns adequately often got handled by a terrifying Black Jail network. This was run by private security 'contractors' who were often little more than underworld thugs loosely mandated by different local governments to deal with people they regarded as trouble-makers. Those who ended up here were often dealt with through violence or threats.

Then there was the simple fact that because the country had undergone immense change in such a short period, it was inevitable it would suffer from trauma and dislocation. Harvard-based Professor of Medical Anthropology Arthur Kleinman and a group of others wrote of a country which was 'more open, modern and highly mobile' but where social trust had declined. In 'Deep China', this new entity which had appeared since reforms had started, there were several kinds of distrust: of the market, owing to faulty goods and bad service, of service providers, friends and relatives, law enforcement officers, and of the law and moral values.[12] The upshot of the many changes in society over recent decades in the PRC was 'the emergence of a new and original Chinese bourgeois culture that centres itself on the outer and interior furnishings of a new Chinese self'.[13] The era of Maoist collectivism was over. Now China, with new technology enabling new networks and new forms of identity, was a place of rampant individualism and hybridity.

Belief systems diversified, with the renaissance of Buddhism, Christianity, folk religions, and, particularly problematic for the government because of its more radical and politicized forms, Islam.

The Era of the Peaceful Rise

WTO entry presaged one very clear phenomenon: the era of Global China had truly arrived. While the country's capital account remained protected, and Chinese currency was unconvertible, in terms of outward and inward investment, and of flows of people and levels of engagement, China became from 2002 to 2012 a place much like the United States, where the line between domestic policy and that of foreign affairs, because of the size and importance of its economy, was almost indecipherable and where even the most domestic issues, from demand for certain goods to economic issues experienced in specific sectors, had global repercussions.

The challenge for the custodians of the great project of national regeneration and renewal around Hu and his fellow leaders was how to craft a message that managed to combine defence of the country's unique political model, still existing despite the predictions of much of the outside world a decade before, along with reassurance that its new economic prominence and the power that flowed from that was a positive, not an ominous, development for the rest of the world.

Hu, with his poor communication skills, was a

highly unusual figure to try to sell this complex message. His visits abroad were striking for their lack of drama and for any kind of sign of charisma by which foreign audiences might be able to relate to this new China now figuring more and more in their lives as a manufacturer, investor, and source of students and tourists. The government response from the early 2000s was to use figures like the retired official Zheng Bijian (1932–) to convey what they wanted the world to understand about their country's emerging role. Zheng crafted a message of 'peaceful rise' – something that paralleled the domestic language of 'harmonious society'. China was a supporter of international systems, as its joining of the WTO had proved. It was also signed up to the War Against Terror after the 11 September 2001 terrorist attacks in the United States. This deflected the two countries from a more confrontational path by uniting them in action against those they considered threats domestically. In China's case, this meant in particular a group of extremists in the Xinjiang region who were accused of being linked to the global radical Islamist movement.

'Peaceful rise' was heavily promoted, even though the notion of a Communist-run country 'rising' was still anathema to many constituents abroad. From 2009, the South China Sea in particular became the site of frequent clashes, usually with fishing vessels, and often involving China and one of the other contesting parties in this area. Their claims were confusing, based often on different interpretations of history and different legal grounds. There were also a number of varying demands being made over different territories, from Vietnam to Malaysia, to the Philippines and even Indonesia. But those of China were the most extensive, stretching down 2,000 kilometres into the Indian Ocean. China's behaviour provoked the Obama administration to insist from 2009 that the United States was a Pacific power, and to prompt the then Secretary of State Hillary Clinton to say that the maritime areas around China were ones of American strategic concern and interest. This in turn prompted the most senior Chinese official dealing specifically with foreign affairs at the time, State Counsellor Dai Bingguo, to talk of Chinese core interests: preservation of the system of one-party rule in the country, and maintenance of a stable environment around it. According to this formulation, the PRC had a vested interest in the South China Sea area and the right to exercise whatever actions it needed there to ensure its interests were protected.

While this did not lead to any large-scale military confrontations, it did create a sense that China was becoming increasingly assertive, and that its silent posture on the global stage was one that could be interpreted as more ominous than welcome. This was despite the fact that the most significant aid to China's rise to global prominence was something it had no direct role in precipitating: the great global financial crisis from 2008 onwards. The source of this was far away from China, in the housing market of the

United States and distortions from that which then spread globally. By the end of 2008, however, and the collapse of a number of prominent banking and financial institutions in Europe and the United States, it was clear that China's main export markets were starting to shrink and that, in order to protect itself, it needed to take action. During the G20 meeting in London in April 2009, it agreed with others a package of new measures to restrain finance from being too adventurous and risk-taking. Back home, the Chinese government implemented a US$600 billion fiscal stimulus package to ensure its own economy did not slow down or go into recession. This resulted in over 10 per cent growth rates in 2010 and 2011. China claimed that it had helped the world avoid the kind of economic catastrophes that had been experienced decades earlier after the 1929 fall of the Stock Exchange in Wall Street. But there were others who said that China's role had in fact indirectly caused the whole crisis in the first place because of the distortions its largely state-led growth model had created.

Political Reform with Chinese Characteristics

In its first full report on China in 2005, the Organization for Economic Co-operation and Development (OECD) stated that one of the most striking developments about the country since 1978 had been that 'the scope of private ownership has become substantial, producing well over half of GDP and an overwhelming share of exports. Private companies generate most new jobs and are improving the productivity and profitability of the whole economy.'[14] The question was what the political significance of these new actors might be. In Russia, after the collapse of the USSR, oligarchs had emerged, shaping the government. Business people had played a major role in the unfolding of the 'Colour Revolutions' in the mid-2000s in states which had broken away from the USSR such as Ukraine, funding new political movements and having an increasingly assertive voice. As with so many other areas, however, things in China developed differently. Jiang Zemin's 'Three Represents' reforms, which allowed entrepreneurs to be Party members (covered in the previous chapter), mitigated the potential threat that the rise of remnimbi and then dollar billionaires in the country represented to the Communist control of its monopoly on organized political power. 'Whereas the popular conception of capitalists portrays them as supporting democratizing reforms and posting an inherent threat to authoritarian regimes,' Jie Chen and Bruce J. Dickson wrote in a study in 2010, 'this has not been the case in China.'[15] Indeed, entrepreneurs seemed to be enthusiastic in becoming Party members, not least because it provided them with networks useful for their business interests.

While business people were seemingly under control, the Party, because of the vastness of its size, remained a source of competition for itself. The fights between those on the more liberal and more conservative side in terms of embracing the market had become less intense since the 1980s, but they had not gone away. In a report written by members of the Central Party School in Beijing, the Communists' chief think tank, economist Zhou Tianyong and a number of other colleagues came out in 2007, before the important Party Congress that year, with a number of ideas. Their starting point was that while everyone agreed that China needed to reform, no one could agree in which direction it should head, and what priority it needed to place on different kinds of reforms. Political ones were the most difficult to judge the impact of and the most complex to implement. There was no question at all, in this report's argument, of contesting the primacy of the Party. What was necessary was to produce more efficient decision-making and have more participation by the public in that. The Party figured in all of this as the source of guidance. This echoed the fact that 'making people the core' was the mantra of the Hu leadership: Chinese Communism with a human face.

Zhou et al.'s suggestions focused on getting more decision-making made locally, by people close to where the impact of these policies would be felt who had more knowledge than remote figures in Beijing. They also argued for more divisions of responsibility, so that, for instance, courts in the legal system would be clearly out of the control of local government, who currently were the ones funding them. They suggested making the role of entities like the National People's

Congress, China's *de facto* parliament (despite having very limited powers), more meaningful by allowing for greater scrutiny of budgets and a reduction in the number of delegates from 3,000 down to around 1,000. They also suggested that new actors in Chinese society, such as business people and non-government organizations, be allowed to have more representation on these bodies.[16]

These proposals were mostly not accepted at the time, though some, such as decentralization of fiscal decision-making, were, after a fashion, pushed forward in the Xi era. What was striking was that even the modest attempt to roll out village multi-candidate elections to township congresses was slowed down, and then by the end of the decade effectively stopped. Talk of election even of Party officials in some locations came, and very quickly went. After a brief period of tolerance in the middle part of the decade, non-government forces and others, particularly those that had received foreign funding, came under increasing political and legal scrutiny. Moves towards transparency in terms of publishing government budgets, and allowing consultations over new laws in draft, were experimented with, but meaningful political reform remained increasingly distant. Indeed, the sole innovation of the Hu era – to have intra-party democracy – carried so little conviction that the idea simply vanished once he left office.

Hu's main ideological contribution was that of the 'scientific outlook on development', a notion written into the Party Constitution in 2007 which stressed sustainability, social welfare, harmony, and humanism. This was somehow meant to give the key tools to confront the large, complex set of issues that have already been referred to in this chapter. It was, in particular, meant to defend the Party as it navigated through a potentially very tricky part of its progress towards fulfilling what Hu called its 'historic mission': the restoration of China to a place of status and global primacy. What is clear is that from 2009 onwards, a number of unexpected external and internal events reinforced the hand of the more conservative elements, and created even more antagonism towards any idea of political reform along Western multi-party lines. The great financial crisis and the large amounts of uncertainty which the aftermath of that produced, referred to above, was one of the most important. But there was also the uprising in Tibet in 2008, followed by the riots that left over 200 dead in Xinjiang the year after, and the disturbances in Inner Mongolia in 2011. All of these reminded Chinese leaders of how precarious their situation might become if they were not perpetually vigilant. The greatest impact of all, however, came from the turbulence experienced in the Middle East with the Arab Spring from 2010, events which, to Chinese onlookers at least, showed that even relatively stable governments, if they did not keep control of dissent, could be swept away overnight.

From 2009 onwards, only one figure in the political elite in China, Premier Wen Jiabao, did make occasional mentions of the need for political reform. But he certainly never spoke of any move towards allowing different political parties in the country to operate and compete for power. While the Xi era is seen as one that has witnessed the most systematic clampdown on dissidents, rights lawyers, and others, the roots of this can be found very well developed in the Hu era.

Olympic Jumps

If a single event captured the contradictions of Hu's China, then this was the 2008 Beijing Olympics. As China lost its bid to stage the 2000 event by only two votes in 1993, its re-application in 2000 was fraught with tense expectation. On the night the successful bid was declared in the capital, there was an explosion of firecrackers and celebration. The preparations for hosting the event itself were complex, and extremely expensive, costing, according to some experts, more than US$49 billion. Large parts of Beijing were rebuilt. Ancient *hutongs* – old alleys dating back centuries with courtyard houses lining them – were knocked down, sometimes despite spirited resistance by local residents. The most important building, that where the opening and closing ceremonies were to be held, was a hugely ambitious, modernist structure partially designed by Ai Weiwei, one of the country's emerging artists. He himself had been a vocal and persistent critic of the government on rights issues. This 'Bird's

Nest Stadium' stood amidst a range of other structures, from swimming pools to cycling stadia.

The massive amounts of money going into what
resembled a rebuild of Beijing were criticized for
being excessive, with some liable to be siphoned away
through corruption. One Vice-Mayor, Liu Zhihua,
had already been felled in 2006 for precisely this
reason. More lower-ranked officials were to be taken
in as the event itself grew closer. But all of this was
exacerbated by a context of rising levels of contention
and conflict. The April uprising in Tibet focused the
eyes of the world on an area the Chinese government
wanted very much kept away from the limelight. In
May, a huge earthquake in Wenquan, Sichuan province, resulted in over 80,000 casualties. While Hu
and his colleagues were applauded immediately after
the catastrophe for the way they had involved foreign
aid organizations, and for the speed of their response,
reporters discovered that many non-government
buildings, from schools to hospitals, had collapsed
owing to their shoddy construction, causing them to
be called 'tofu' structures on account of their softness.
Defensive responses to these criticisms by officials only
added fuel to the fire. Critics of China were also able
to refer to significant issues in relation to the country's behaviour in Africa, with arms supply to Omar
al-Bashir's government engaged in a vicious civil war
in Sudan amongst the most criticized. Chinese arms
shipments to Robert Mugabe's regime in Zimbabwe,
meanwhile, were stopped by dock workers while

transiting in South Africa. The accumulation of Tibet, Africa, and Wenquan meant that by the summer, calls were occurring for a boycott of the opening ceremony. The label 'Genocide' Olympics was bandied around. Within China, angry and resentful nationalism from some quarters pushed back. There were fears that the 8 August opening ceremony would be a fiasco.

Beijing 2008, nevertheless, ended up being a success, at least domestically: a moment heavy with symbolism, as significant for what it omitted as for what it contained. Reference to Mao Zedong was conspicuously absent throughout the opening night. In hindsight, however, the event was pregnant with the new meanings that a wealthy China was now presenting both to itself and to the world. It was a declaration of intent, though one that no one knew quite what to make of at the time. Through its conspicuous materialism and the celebration of a life of consumption and greater and greater riches, nothing seen on stage in 2008 would have been regarded as overtly Communist – and yet the very organization of the event and the military precision that lay behind it evidently came from a system that privileged the collective over the individual and emanated from a ruling entity that had the power and resources to make people obey its will. Confidence was one side of the 2008 festival. But another was excess, lack of moral discipline, and corruption. China was in great danger of over-gorging on itself, and falling into complacency and self-regard at a moment when it should have been even more tightly focused on the potential great prize before it: the realization of its modern dream to be a great, powerful country, not just put on shows that presented this as a fantasy.

China's Conscience: Liu Xiaobo

Worrying about China has a long and distinguished history in the country. As historian Gloria Davies has argued, 'Worrying about the problems that prevent China from attaining perfection, not only as a nation, but also as an enduring civilization, is the kind of patriotic sentiment one commonly encounters in the essays of Chinese intellectuals.' More pertinently, such worrying (in Chinese, *youhuan*) is a 'call to duty from which Chinese intellectuals have traditionally drawn their critical inquiry.'[17]

Liu Xiaobo (1955–2017), a gifted writer, intellectual, and thinker, was one of the figures who worried about China in a very particular way as it progressed towards its dream of great nation status based on material wealth and power. Liu had been active since the 1989 uprising. His main targets had been Party officials who had been consumed by greed and selfishness while robotically parroting lines from a Marxist ideology they clearly no longer either understood or cared about. The hypocrisy and hollowness of contemporary Chinese cultural and political existence, the refusal to undertake a systematic debunking of Mao and his legacy, and the general materialism of life in contemporary China, with its underlying confusion, sense of emptiness, and nihilism – all of these figured in Liu's powerful essays. It was the rising tide of nationalism, however, that particularly caught his attention. The Hu era, with its multiple challenges and the complex conditions it was facing in society, some of them described in this chapter, placed increasing importance on resolving this by simply arguing that everything that was happening would be eventually justified by living in a country that was great and powerful. The myth of a China that was singular, united within itself, and the product of a particular, almost linear, history was central to this. Liu labelled this 'thuggish and bellicose patriotism'. Its characteristics were:

(1) A history of feeling disdain for the world and a powerful feeling of vanity that the Son of Heaven once ruled All Under Heaven;

(2) A long history of having suffered humiliation at the hands of foreigners and the building of popular sentiment for revenge and settling scores;

(3) Pressure of people's livelihood because of an extremely large population and natural resources that are insufficient to support it;

(4) Rising diplomatic and military power in the present day;

(5) A solid record over an extended time of education-for-hatred in school curricula and the misleading of public opinion in controlled media;

(6) A national psychology that regularly alternates between extreme self-abasement and extreme self-aggrandisement; and

(7) A dictatorial regime that can manipulate the aggregate power of the preceding six conditions.[18]

These were sobering reflections for the outside world to take on board. They also proved unpalatable to the Chinese elite leadership. Liu's role in drafting a manifesto for political change in 2008, Charter 08, had resulted in his incarceration the following year, and an eleven-year sentence. In 2010, he was awarded the Nobel Prize for Peace, presented to an empty chair because of his inability to attend the Oslo ceremony. Liu was to tragically die seven years later of cancer. But his diagnosis of the darker side of the Chinese dream remains particularly potent in the era in which that dream has become so much more compelling, both within China and outside.

8

China's Dream Realized under Xi Jinping?

The leadership transition from Hu to Xi was the cleanest and clearest in PRC history. Hu left all positions by March 2013, moving completely into retirement. At this point, his successor, Xi Jinping (1953–), had already accrued a formidable cluster of titles: Party Secretary, Chair of the Central Military Commission, and President. In the ensuing years, he was to bolster this with further embellishments. In late 2016, he had core status within the leadership conferred on him by the Party – something Hu had desisted from.[1] He was also appointed to head a number of Small Leading Groups, the main bodies within the Party which made core policy decisions and which put critical parts of the bureaucratic, political, and governance apparatus together. This won him the label 'Chairman of Everything'.[2] In an era in which the Party was meant to be more about institution building than focusing on just one person, and where the revulsion by wide parts of society at the Rule of Man rather than the Rule of Law in the Mao era was still strong, this was unusual behaviour. Deng Xiaoping had exercised vast and enduring influence with no formal positions from 1982 beyond that of chairing the Central Military Commission till 1989. Jiang had had the top three positions, as had Hu – but for both there had been a sense of them operating in an environment where figures like Zhu Rongji or Wen Jiabao were also extremely influential. They were presented as being 'first among equals'. The rule of the Party corporately was what mattered.

With Xi, a striking characteristic of his period in power to the time of writing (spring 2020) has been the stress on uniformity: in leadership, in policy, and in governance. The outside world, and some critics within the country, have seen this as a new kind of Maoism: autocracy enabled by a technological super-state that can see further and do more than ever before. One of the most prominent critical voices has been an academic based at Tsinghua University in Beijing, the legal scholar Xu Zhangrun, whose lengthy essay from 2018, 'Imminent Fears, Immediate Hopes', defends, in a manner similar to some of the Big Character Posters protesting during the latter part of the CR and the Democracy Wall campaign, and the writings of Liu Xiaobo, basic principles of develop-ment, freedom, and openness which are once more under attack. 'Yet again,' Xu wrote, 'people throughout China – including the entire bureaucratic class – are feeling a sense of uncertainty, a mounting anxiety in relation both to the direction the country is taking as well as in regard to their personal security.' And while his essay also lists after its diagnosis some grounds for optimism (the 'eight hopes', as he puts it, eight being a particularly auspicious number in Chinese), his reward for this candour was to lose his job the following year.[3]

Voices like Xu's are rare. The Xi era has seen a remarkable consolidation of Party message and power, and an expansion of the influence and power attributed to the key leader. The use of a particular narrative lies at the heart of this, one about a country that is now emerging from its modern history to take up its position once more as no longer a victim, or weak, or marginalized, but at the heart of world affairs. The potency of this message is reinforced by the sense that it is accompanied by tangible developments justifying this sense of mission and historic realization, actions and happenings people can see, rather than hopes and aspirations projected to occur in the distant future. Xi may gain his powers from many different sources and places, but they all derive from one root: the China Dream that he talks about so frequently and which the Party he leads is said to represent. That, in essence, is the true power that runs China today.

China's Dreaming

Strategically, getting the message right at the start means that everything else follows smoothly from this. Xi and his colleagues spent much time on this task from the very first day of his becoming Party leader in mid-November 2012. His comments that day set the tone:

> Ours is a great nation. Throughout 5,000 years of
> development, the Chinese nation has made signifi-
> cant contributions to the progress of human civiliza-
> tion. Since the advent of modern times, our nation
> has gone through untold tribulations and faced its
> greatest perils. Countless people with lofty ideals rose
> up for the rejuvenation of the Chinese nation.[4]

In the past, China had all too often failed to realize
its potential. But not under the CPC, which, since
its foundation, had led 'poor and backward China
into an increasingly prosperous and strong nation,
thus opening completely new horizons for national
rejuvenation'. 'Rejuvenation' has become one of the
keywords of Xi-era discourse ever since. It has been
associated with a consistent iconography and set of
symbols too, ones that have been promoted by the
Party ideologues and propagandists. Within a few
weeks of taking power, Xi visited Shenzhen, one of
the sacred sites for reform and opening up, connecting himself to the Deng Xiaoping narrative of Party
development. But he also ensured that the Maoist tradition was not forgotten, appearing and speaking at a
symposium to celebrate the 120th anniversary of the
Chairman's birth in late December 2012. 'People,' he
declared there, 'are the creators of history.'[5]

The quintessential combination of venue, occasion,
and language occurred right at the end of the year,
when, Xi spoke at an exhibition held in the National
Museum of China. Standing on the eastern side of

Tiananmen Square, this vast building had been one of the key modern Soviet-inspired structures erected in the 1950s (others had included the Great Hall of the People facing it). At the display, 'The Road to Rejuvenation', flanked by his six other Standing Committee members, Xi had talked of 'the China Dream': rejuvenation. 'Our struggles in the last 170 years since the Opium War have created bright prospects for achieving the rejuvenation of the Chinese nation,' he declared. 'We are now closer to this goal, and more confident and capable of achieving it than at any time in history.'[6] Everyone has a dream, he went on. 'We are now talking about the Chinese Dream. In my opinion, achieving the rejuvenation of the Chinese nation has been the greatest dream of Chinese people since the advent of modern times.'[7] Now it was real, and happening. In the Hu era, the leadership had maintained a commitment to narrowly technocratic language, with next to no space for talking of ideals, aspirations, and expectations beyond those that could be captured in a statistic. For the new era, however, with its special qualities and the spectre of imminent revival, ideals and hopes, and dreams, could make a comeback. In the era of Mao, such notions had had disastrous outcomes. But now things would be different. It was alright, Xi was saying, to hope and dream in China – as long as you did it in unison with the Party!

Around the time that Xi spoke publicly about the China Dream, he also made clear to Politburo colleagues and other leaders that the country needed to proactively tell its own story. While not framed as such, this was an indirect criticism of the Hu era, where silence had been the order of the day. Xi took the lead on this mission of storytelling, using his own biography in ways which Hu, with his love of anonymity and impersonality, had never tried to do. In drawing on his own life story, Xi has stressed his experiences in the Chinese countryside, and how he had worked up through the lowest to the highest levels of government. He is a leader who, the implicit message is, understands people. He is not remote like leaders sometimes have appeared to be in the past, but someone whom Chinese can relate to. Xi's story is the story of the average Chinese citizen: someone who had to undergo tribulation and suffering, but who believes profoundly in the Party rejuvenation mission and derives authenticity and legitimacy from this. Such a narrative avoids some of the more complex elements of his biography: why he took over ten attempts to join the CPC in the early 1970s; what he really thinks of Mao Zedong, despite being so often compared to him, a person who was responsible for his own father's long period in detention, and who overshadowed his own childhood; and how it is that someone keen to stress their grass-roots experience had a first marriage to the daughter of a key diplomat, and after divorcing her married one of the most famous singers in modern China, Peng Liyuan.

Rejuvenation Starts at Home: Cleansing the Party

From 2012, the Party had a refreshed and revivified story to tell the nation. But there was little use in this without the entity telling this story at least having credibility. At this critical time, when China's moment of rejuvenation was so close – it had been mapped out in the two centennial goals of 2021 to mark the hundredth anniversary of the foundation of the Communist Party, and 2049 for that of the PRC – there was an awareness that the biggest threat to the Party fulfilling its great objectives could be itself. This had been present from the very start of the Deng reforms in the 1980s. But by Hu's era, as the economic growth levels boomed, so too did the disparity between the relatively modest wages of officials and the billions of remnimbi involved in the infrastructure and other projects for which they had decision-making responsibility. Political scientist Andrew Wedeman refers to something inherently contradictory in this situation: a China where corruption on most measures was worsening, and yet there was continuing rapid growth. He calls this the 'double paradox of corruption and growth'.[8] Perhaps an explanation of this is simply that growth was so rampant in post-WTO China that levels of corruption were an unwanted, but inevitable, side-effect of all of this. Who really cared if officials were on the take when everyone was getting richer and richer, and no one had time to keep tabs on what others were doing?

The great cleansing that Xi's leadership undertook from 2013 was principally aimed at addressing the crisis of Party image at a time when it needed to have leaders with at least some moral authority. This was a hard task. The anti-corruption struggle, headed by the formidable Wang Qishan (1947–), waged targeted campaigns first against the Party itself, then against different ministries and state enterprises, and finally against business people. With massive, and much feared, extrajudicial powers, the Central Commission for Discipline and Inspection (CCDI) took the unprecedented step of prosecuting former members of the Standing Committee of the Politburo like Zhou Yongkang, figures like Ling Jihua, who had been a key adviser to Hu Jintao, and those in the top levels of the military. In 2017, before the Congress that year, rising star Sun Zhengcai was toppled. So too were key figures in the energy and petroleum sector. Even the first Chinese to be appointed head of Interpol, Meng Hongwei, was detained on a visit back to his native land from Paris, where he was based, and placed under interrogation. No one was immune.

Speculation that the causes behind this were more about Xi removing his political foes than about really addressing corruption per se were rife. The campaign did succeed in creating such levels of fear in the Party that almost all signs of dissent vanished. But making sure that the Party was utterly united as China marched on its mission of rejuvenation towards 2021 and beyond was more likely the larger intention. A report by the CCDI in 2018 stated that it had handled 1.54 million cases, involving 1.53 million cadres. Of these, 58,000 were transferred to the judiciary for formal trial, double that of the previous five years.[9]

An extensive, sustained drive like this may have created high levels of anxiety within the governing and business elite, but it proved to be good populist politics. Xi's role in the Party and nationally soon became uncontested – so much so that even a move as provocative as that in 2018 to remove constitutional limits on the time one person could serve as President met only *sotto voce* protest. Xi's ambitions for the newly cleansed, morally refreshed Party took over three hours to spell out during his key speech at the Ninteenth Party Congress in October 2017. The Party, he could say, was engaged in partnership with the Chinese people on an historic mission, and this justified the brutality of the anti-corruption struggle, and the removal of some surprising figures. As with Mao, the calculus was that the ends justified the means.

China's World

China's Dream was the domestic vision sold by the Xi leadership. This had a parallel narrative which was displayed to the outside world. Unlike the 'Dream', the external story took some time to evolve. But it, too, was aimed at filling in the gap that had appeared during the Hu era where China had become increasingly important, and visible, as an economic actor and yet seemed to have no voice with which to speak to the world and answer some of its questions and concerns.

One idea that evidently appealed to the Xi leadership came from the academic Wang Jisi, and writings he had produced from the Hu era about the need to internationalize the opening up to the West of the decade before, and concentrate on China's land borders rather than those facing the sea. Here there was potential to solve the country's problem of being so dependent on sea routes largely controlled by the United States and its powerful navy. Central Asia was complex and unstable, but it did supply an alternative, if the approach was right. Robert S. Ross has written of how China's geopolitical traditions through much of modern history had been those of a country that is 'a continental power' which 'reflects geography but also the culture of a land power'. He goes on to explain that 'Chinese development of a navy has been, at best, brief and sporadic.'[10] Ironically, at a time when it was now developing a major naval capacity, its land borders became more significant. They offered access to new economic opportunities and a new set of partners. These were all there to be explored, and perhaps exploited, in the era of Global China.

In 2013, Xi started to make reference to the New Silk Road. The ancient Silk Road, whatever its historical veracity, was something that at least the outside world had some notion of. It was sensible to build on that, referring to a time hundreds of years ago when the Tang and Han had been major empires, with trade links, both direct and indirect, that ran throughout the world. The Silk Road was also presented as a route for ideas, into and out of China: the conduit through which Buddhism had come into the Tang, and artefacts that embodied Chinese civilization, like silk, calligraphy, and language, had made their way out into the wider world. Speaking in September 2013 in Astana, Kazakhstan, and then a few weeks later in Jakarta, Indonesia, Xi referred to not just a land economic belt, but a maritime road. In 2015, this became the 'One Belt, One Road', and the following year the more user-friendly 'Belt and Road Initiative' (BRI).

The BRI was the key part of the Xi-era story to the outside world. As such, it performed a number of functions. Its principal articulations within China were along the lines of producing different kinds of connectivity with the country's land and sea neighbours. That meant logistics, finance, internet and communications, cultural understanding, and flows of people doing business and as tourists. But these were part of the ingredients of an idea that was specifically designed to evolve, not be prescriptive, and answer questions about the nature of Chinese power which did not frighten off or intimidate an external audience. China, after all, even in the era of Xi, still needed the outside world to continue its development, if not as a market, then as a place where Chinese power was validated and affirmed. What was the point of being a great power and having status if the only audience for this was oneself?

The BRI therefore took a number of guises. It was first of all the story that China wanted to tell its immediate region. This was a very tough neighbourhood to be in. Russia, North Korea, Mongolia, Pakistan, India, Vietnam, Myanmar, Afghanistan, Laos: all these countries with their different cultures, belief systems, languages, and often fractious and complex histories with China, some stretching back over hundreds of years, were watching their massive neighbour's rise with a mixture of excitement (Pakistan, one of China's most stalwart allies) and deep apprehension (India, still unable to resolve a border dispute with the PRC). The BRI was an invitation from China to its neighbours to develop themselves with its help, but also to become more involved with the rise of a Chinese middle class with large spending capacity. As a quasi-common economic zone, this appealed to everyone's self-interests. It avoided complex issues about politics and security, at least at the start, and kept things simple by focusing on aid projects, exports and imports, and the potential of Chinese finance now that it was becoming a larger foreign investor.

The BRI was also a means of China exporting its development model, and, through entities like the Asian Infrastructure Investment Bank, working more with others to show them how they might be able to adapt and use some of the ideas that the PRC had employed since 1978 in unleashing growth and delivering people from poverty.

The BRI was also a means whereby China was able to solve some of its supply route issues, diversifying its energy sources from the Middle East and Central Asia by creating the rail and road infrastructure that could bring these to China. In reverse, it also created new export markets to compensate for the decline of those in more mature destinations previously well favoured like Europe or the United States. The BRI provided a context within which China had greater control over its own narratives, speaking to audiences in Pakistan, Myanmar, Cambodia, and elsewhere who were less negatively predisposed towards the country simply because of its unique political model. Unsurprisingly, Confucius Institutes, set up partially with Chinese government money, sprang up along some of the major routeways of the BRI.

This did not mean that geopolitics was absent from the whole vast notion. Far from it. With the BRI, China was sending a clear declaration to the wider world that it did not want to become a second America, following in the sole surviving superpower's footsteps. Part of the reason for this is that Xi was careful in making sure that, just like Deng and other leaders before him, he did not stoke the jealousy of the United States by any overt signs of wanting to one day usurp or overtake it. America was still a potent cultural and military force, and likely to remain so for many decades into the future. Even the surprise election of the more isolationist President Trump in Washington in late 2016 did not change this calculation. China definitely did not want direct confrontation. Its designs were more subtle. Using an idea like the BRI, it desired instead to be a new kind of power. As Yan Xuetong of Tsinghua University stated, 'The goal of [China's] strategy must be not only to reduce the power gap with the United States but also to provide a better model for society than that given by the United States.'[11]

This was a bold aim. For fellow academics in China, a more modest objective was needed. 'In its foreign policy,' Xu Jin argued, 'China lacks a universal moral ideal or high point. China still lacks what can attract the countries of the world to naturally follow it.'[12] And for Yang Qianrui, 'Our problem, both now and far into the future, is to guarantee our own survival, development and security, not lead the world.'[13] Deng Xiaoping had urged China to be modest, helpful, and not to seek hegemony or leadership except when absolutely forced to. The BRI therefore stressed partnership, mutual gain, and was presented as the opposite of a more US-style idea of 'leading from the front'. It was all about creating, in Asia and elsewhere, a community of shared destiny.

Despite these efforts, the BRI attracted plenty of criticisms. It was accused of being a means by which to saddle less developed countries with debt. A port in Sri Lanka had to be made over to Chinese ownership because of problems servicing these obligations in 2019. BRI projects were accused of involving export of Chinese labour and not helping the local economies. India and Russia, for different reasons, and in different ways, watched nervously as the initiative expanded. America and Japan categorically refused to sign up to it in the first place. For some it typified the statist nature of the Chinese economy and development philosophy, and allowed the country to export its lack of legal understanding, and its economic distortions, to the world around it. In Indonesia, BRI projects were accused of being heedless of local labour and environmental laws. In other places like Pakistan they created expectations which were hard to satisfy. China itself acquired assets and interest via the initiative in places with high levels of insecurity and instability, meaning that despite the stress on the BRI being purely about commerce and trade flows, private security contractors had to be employed to protect Chinese workers and interests. With the writing of the BRI into the State Constitution in 2017, the one thing that could be said about the project was that it was likely to persist, just because the issue it tried to address – China's role in the world – was also one that would not disappear. The question was how and in what ways it would develop and evolve.

Social Life in the China Dream

Imposition of social control in the Hu era had been scrappy, despite the consistent harshness shown towards any dissidents and critics who crossed the most serious red line: challenging the legitimacy of the Party to a monopoly on organized political power. Under Xi, however, any expectations of liberalization were quickly dispelled. At a Party meeting in late 2013, a commitment was made to developing the rule of law, but in a framework where commercial rules were strengthened and civil and criminal ones remained highly politicized. The Party, having learned lessons from the key actors in the Colour Revolutions and Arab Spring, was not about to open up spaces for activist lawyers, journalists, and nongovernmental groups. These, especially those with known links to international partners, were to enter one of the most restrictive times in modern Chinese history post-1978.

Rights lawyers were amongst the most harshly treated, with over 250 being 'detained' in 2015, and a few handed harsh sentences for state subversion. During a visit to the China Central Television studios the following year, Xi demanded the same loyalty from the journalists as he had from his own party's members and the military. The key thing was to tell China's story, to remain unified, be responsible, and support the nation as it continued its great patriotic mission. An instruction in a formal government document at the start of 2013, called 'Document Number 9', demanded that academics not promote Western political, legal, and social ideals in the classroom. For dissidents, any attempt to disseminate their ideas, or to organize, was met with swift and decisive action.

The Beijing government's defence of this was that it had the right to defend itself against domestic security threats, and there were radical Islamist groups that had mounted campaigns in China, from the horrific Kunming train station massacre in 2014 to a suicide bomb in Tiananmen Square later the same year. The gargantuan scale of what was happening in the north-western Xinjiang region, however, home to the Turkic Uyghur minority, seemed to exceed any possible justification on the grounds of these and other attacks. A grid-pattern network where there were police stations every hundred or so metres in urban centres, and multiple restrictions on what people could wear, carry, and how they could behave, were supplemented by a campaign led by Party officials at a local level who would maintain daily visits on families they were assigned responsibility for. Claims of brainwashing, torture, human rights abuses, and immense levels of misery in the region impacted badly on China's global reputation. This was accompanied by an increasingly hardening attitude towards Taiwan when the independence-leaning Tsai Ing-wen was voted in as President in 2016. The logic of national rejuvenation dictated that Taiwan, as the final left-over issue from history, somehow had to be swept into the narrative of China's unified rebirth. The blockage here was the slight matter of 23 million Taiwanese who after almost seven decades of *de facto* independence and separation from the Mainland begged to disagree.

By far and away the most important group for Xi, however, were not dissidents, Party members, foreign observers, or even business people, but the great emerging middle class. These were the people who took centre stage. They were the engine of the new economic model the country was trying to create. Most now lived in cities, and the majority worked in services, which constituted over 55 per cent of all economic activity by 2018. Their consumption was low, but rising, and held the key to where in the future the country might be able to continue decent GDP development as manufacturing for export and the gains from that started to wear off. In the past, the China model was built with the blood, sweat, and tears of the migrant labour force. Cheap labour was what China had most of. But in the era of Xi, with 7 million university graduates from the country's 2,500 universities, many of them, like Tsinghua and Beida, rising rapidly up the global ranking tables, it was the property-owning, office- or business-working, finance-savvy middle class who mattered most. These numbered 300 million in 2017. They were likely to increase to double this in the next decade, although, for economic rather than social reasons, they tended to have single-child families, despite relaxations on China's One-Child Policy from 2016. They were the people who invested on the Shanghai Stock Exchange, and whom Xi and his colleagues had to protect from a major collapse by state intervention in 2015 and early 2016. They were the people who were still keen to buy luxury brands, from cars to handbags, despite the hefty tariffs the state slapped on these items. They constituted a significant proportion of the 140 million tourists who left China to travel abroad in 2018 alone. These people were the beneficiaries of the anti-corruption clampdown because they were the audience that officials needed to be more responsive and respectful towards. They were the people who were being appealed to with the legal reform changes in 2013 mentioned above, because these at least protected their property and commercial rights. These people were not protestors; they were patriotic, hardworking, but also highly demanding. They wanted better food, better services, better social welfare, and a better standard of life. They were the group that Xi with his Dream and his message of national rejuvenation needed to keep happy. And they were the group that he had most reason to fear if anything about the great project of China's renaissance came unstuck.

A Happy Ending?

From the end of the Qing, when intellectuals and others were wrestling with what to make of their country's experiences of humiliation and victimization at the hands of others, and when there was a feeling of almost perpetual decline, to the Republican era, with its hybrid model of modernity inspired by Sun Yatsen, right into the Communist period, the one constant across the very different political structures has been a commitment to a strong, rich China, a place that needed to be redeemed and did not deserve the parlous position that it had been placed in.

This same task could be said to be the most important one for the five key leaders who have been in control of the PRC since 1949. Despite their very different personalities, interests, and outlooks, Mao Zedong, Deng Xiaoping, Jiang Zemin, Hu Jintao, and Xi Jinping are united by their commitment to a nationalist vision promoted by a Communist ideology. While never declared explicitly, Marxism-Leninism almost functions in their calculus not as an end in itself, bringing about an ideal society, but as a means to something they heretically believe matters much more: a resurgent, great, powerful China, restored at last to its central place in the world.

The imperative to achieve this mission is one that has guided all the various leaders China has had in the last hundred years. But the means they have used in order to achieve this have radically differed. Part of the reason for this was their varying interpretations of why China had fallen so far behind in terms of modernization and industrialization. A victim mentality went hand in hand with either over-exaggeration of the powers of foreigners, or underestimation of them. For Chiang Kai-shek, China's ills were the fault of foreign interference. For Mao, it was more a case of seeking enemies within. His social experiments were to take a heavy toll on the country, just as much as Chiang's divisive and sometimes virulent campaigns to enforce

Nationalist rule ended up in the late 1940s being self-defeating. Ironically, it was the less dramatic Deng who finally found a balance, trying to work with the world, gain from relations internationally, but always with an eye to China's benefit. For all the differences in style and approach between Xi and Deng, it is the framework created by Deng that China still adheres to. And Deng proved himself to be the provider of the most effective implementation of the nationalistic vision, because he managed to bridge the great divide between a China isolated by its own self-sufficient cultural and intellectual uniqueness, and one that at least openly admitted it needed to learn something from the world around it and managed to find a balanced way to do this.

From the late 1970s, reform as a concept always had a productive ambiguity about it. It was fundamentally critical of the Maoist approach to society, economics, and even politics, without ever having the discourtesy of stating this too openly. It also allowed for some searching criticisms of where China had come to, proposals for how it needed to fundamentally change, and reappraisals of its role in the world. Reform institutionalized and internalized dissatisfaction with the current state of China. It shifted the focus away from an almost narcissistic self-satisfaction with just being Chinese, and asked more productive questions about what it meant to say one was Chinese, and how this related to modernity and modernization. There was an eventual move, ongoing to this day, of reconciling China's complex historical traditions and diverse thought systems with this narrative of modernity, rather than sundering them, as the Mao era had tried to do. The Xi era is only the most recent, and most sophisticated, attempt to achieve this. Mao had tried, and in the end failed, to bury tradition. Under Xi, tradition is being renewed and made a crucial part of the overall design of a path to renaissance.

As renewal becomes actual, and manifests itself in the lives of Chinese people, their status in the world, and the way that China as a country shapes those around it, there will be even larger changes than the ones we have already seen. Of these, the most profound will be, at least for the Party, how it shifts its creed from one which has served it so well of being on a mission to achieving this new status, to one that has to now preserve, defend, and embellish it. For the Party in the century in which it has existed, the future has always been a great asset: a place where hopes and dreams could reside, the focus of all effort and attention, containing the good things that justified the current suffering and sacrifices. Developed countries like the United Kingdom, or France, or Germany – they all had pasts. They were just trying to preserve the good things they had. The United States was forever in the present, still enjoying the American Dream. But China, on a more epic scale and more dramatically than anyone else, had a Future: a place where it could fulfil the potential that had never properly been realized in its often harrowing modern history. That gave the country an ambition and hunger, and a dynamism, that served it well. Everyone was waiting for the next chapter. The story was always going forwards. There were no lulls, no moments for static contemplation and rest. Socialism with Chinese characteristics meant perpetual forward momentum and onward-directed energy.

Now, though, it is not the perils of forever forging forward that are greatest, but what happens when the most important thing in the future – the creation of a strong and unified China – becomes no longer an aspiration but a fact. How does the Party shift its attention from creating this to the less exciting option of responsibly preserving it? And what does it do to mobilize people when its greatest asset – hope about the future and fulfilment of historic goals – disappears. Ideology doesn't attract Chinese people – Marxism-Leninism barely registers with them. And there are many episodes in the Party's history that a period of contemplation would make very problematic: the famines, the CR, the purges from its earliest period to today. Once its promise of renewing China is brought to pass, and actually exists, what is the Party's core message then? It has achieved what it promised. Shouldn't some other system or other players have a chance to come in now? All these questions and options that the Party put on hold during the period of urgent transformation and special measures are no longer so easy to deal with. The simple reality is that modern history shows us at least one thing: political ideologies and practices such as Communism come and will probably go; but Chinese nationalism looks likely to be here to stay.

Further Reading

For general histories of modern China, *The Rise of Modern China* (Oxford: Oxford University Press, 2000, Sixth Edition) by Immanuel C. Y. Hsu is authoritative, and runs from the transition between the Ming and the Qing in the seventeenth century to the return of Hong Kong in 1997. As its title suggests, *The Search for Modern China* (London and New York: Hutchinson, 1990) by Jonathan D. Spence, while covering roughly the same period as Hsu, focuses more on the country's struggle with modernity, through the Qing and into the Republican and then Communist periods. Jonathan Fenby's *The Penguin History of Modern China: The Fall and Rise of a Great Power* (London and New York: Allen Lane, 2008) is a well-written, well-structured narrative account. *The Cambridge History of China*, Vol. 14, *The People's Republic, Part 1: The Emergence of Revolutionary China 1949–1965* and *Part 2: Revolution within the Chinese Revolution 1966–1982*, edited by Roderick MacFarquhar and John K. Fairbank (Cambridge: Cambridge University Press, 1987 and 1991, respectively), has largely chronologically ordered, detailed, and granular accounts of the key events in the Maoist and immediate post-Maoist period. On China's often tortured relations with the outside world, an accessible and credible account can be found in Odd Arne Westad's *Restless Empire: China and the World since 1750* (London: Bodley Head, 2012). On the Qing and its rise and slow, tragic decline, William T. Rowe's *China's Last Empire: The Great Qing* (Cambridge, Mass., and London: Belknap Press of Harvard University Press, 2009) is concise and approaches the 260-year history of the final great dynasty thematically, with chapters on society, commerce, and revolution, among other areas.

The endlessly complex issue of national identity is explored from a Chinese perspective by the contemporary historian Ge Zhaoquang in *What is China? Territory, Ethnicity, Culture and History* (trans. Matthew Gibbs Hill, Cambridge, Mass.: Belknap Press of Harvard University Press, 2018). Ge is unafraid to struggle with big concepts and lay out some clear intellectual commitments which, because they are based on deep and long scholarship, merit serious attention, whatever conclusions the reader might ultimately draw themselves. A very different approach, at least intellectually, is offered by Prasenjit Duara in *Rescuing History from the Nation: Questioning Narratives of Modern China* (Chicago: University of Chicago Press, 1995), which sets about the business, as the title suggests, of deconstructing the nationalist rationale of contemporary retellings of China's history and their frequent politicization.

On the important question of what sense to make of Chinese history, and what frameworks to see it within, at least in modern times, then W. J. F. Jenner's *The Tyranny of History: The Roots of China's Crisis* (London: Allen Lane, 1992) offers useful orientation. Its core argument of the great burden that China's long and multiple pasts can present to those of Chinese identity still has elements that are relevant and useful today, despite the ways in which much of that history has been reconfigured by patriotic and nationalist campaigns of the 1990s and is now regarded as an asset rather than an impediment. While focusing on the Cultural Revolution era, Mobo Gao's *The Battle for China's Past: Mao and the Cultural Revolution* (Ann Arbor, Mich., and London: Pluto Press, 2008) is a spirited attempt at revisionism, offering a defence of Maoist politics and the movement they are now closely connected to, and denounced for. Mark Elvin's two books, *The Pattern of the Chinese Past* (Stanford: Stanford University Press, 1973) and *Changing Stories in the Chinese World* (Stanford: Stanford University Press, 1997), weave literature, history, and social science together, drawing on sources from modern and pre-modern Chinas, addressing the issues that Jenner and Gao also approach but in a more orthodox, academic manner. They are still very pleasurable to read, despite this. On moral narratives and the philosophy of history that the Communist Party embraced from 1949, see Kerry Brown's *China's Dreams: The Culture of the Communist Party and the Secret Source of Its Power* (Cambridge: Polity, 2018). Lucian W. Pye's works on the leadership culture of the Communist Party and how it tended to be grafted on to much more ancient governance philosophies can be found in *The Mandarin and the Cadre* (Ann Arbor, Mich.: Center for Chinese Studies, 1988) where he coins the memorable phrase 'Confucian Leninism' to describe the situation after 1949.

Definitive editions of the works of Mao Zedong continue to be produced, in English and Chinese. But a taster of the Chairman at his most direct and confronting can be found in *Mao Tse-Tung Unrehearsed: Talks and Letters 1956–71* (Harmondsworth: Penguin Books, 1974), edited by the late Stuart Schram. Studies of Mao can often be challenging because of the habit they have of being either hagiographic or uniformly condemnatory. They can also get quickly sunk in complexity because of the epic quality of Mao's life. Philip Short's *Mao: A Life* (London: Hodder & Stoughton, 1999), like his equally impressive biography of Cambodia's Pol Pot, has the invaluable merit of being straightforward and neutral. That of Alexander V. Pantsov and Steven I. Levine, *Mao: The Real Story* (New York and London: Simon & Schuster, 2012), is real in the sense that it draws on Russian archival material in ways which at least give detail unavailable before about what direct contact with the Communist leader of the PRC was like.

Of the key leaders since Mao, Deng has inevitably been best served. Ezra F. Vogel's *Deng Xiaoping and the Transformation of China* (Cambridge, Mass., and London: Belknap Press of Harvard University Press,

2011) is the most meticulous, though of its 700 pages, fewer than 50 cover the years 1904 to 1969. This means that Alexander V. Pantsov and Steven I. Levine's *Deng Xiaoping: A Revolutionary Life* (Oxford: Oxford University Press, 2015), again through use of Russian archives, addresses the paramount leader's earlier career in much more detail. Michael Dillon's *Deng Xiaoping: The Man Who Made Modern China* (London: I. B. Tauris, 2015) is able to produce interesting source material from Deng's years in France in the 1920s. For Hu Jintao, Kerry Brown's *Hu Jintao: China's Silent Ruler* (Singapore: World Scientific, 2012) is one of the few comprehensive studies of a man who often appeared as if he wanted to come across with no past. For Xi Jinping, Willy Wo-Lap Lam's *Chinese Politics in the Era of Xi Jinping: Renaissance, Reform or Retrogression?* (London and New York: Routledge, 2015) appeared at a time when it was not yet clear that the Xi era would be a combination of all three. Kerry Brown's *CEO China: The Rise of Xi Jinping* (London and New York: I. B. Tauris, 2016) looks at Xi's earlier career, and some of his writings while a provincial and then central leader.

On the Chinese economy and its development since 1949, while simply enormous amounts of material have been produced, inside and outside China, on every conceivable aspect of the country's development, the clearest work for non-specialists remains the excellent comprehensive overview by Barry Naughton, *The Chinese Economy: Transitions and Growth* (Cambridge, Mass.: MIT Press, 2007). This can be supplemented by *China's Economy: What Everyone Needs to Know* (Oxford: Oxford University Press, 2016) by Arthur R. Kroeber, which covers key issues in the era of Xi up to 2015.

For useful and stimulating accounts of the PRC as it has evolved since 1949, the two books by Ralph A. Thaxton Jr, *Catastrophe and Contention in Rural China: Mao's Great Leap Forward Famine and the Origins of Righteous Resistance in Da Fo Village* (Cambridge: Cambridge University Press, 2008) and *Force and Contention in Contemporary China: Memory and Resistance in the Long Shadow of the Catastrophic Past* (Cambridge: Cambridge University Press, 2016), are models of how to write about modern Chinese history in ways which are respectful of the human tragedies being recounted, but also do so on a scale which remains accessible rather than numbing. Despite its focus on elite political dynamics and the often deeply unattractive case of characters being described, Roderick MacFarquhar and Michael Schoenhals's *Mao's Last Revolution* (Cambridge, Mass.: Belknap Press of Harvard University Press, 2006) is surprisingly easy to read. It should, however, be compared with works like *Maoism at the Grassroots: Everyday Life in China's Era of High Socialism*, edited by Jeremy Brown and Matthew D. Johnson (Cambridge, Mass.: Harvard University Press, 2015), which pays attention with excellent use of new source material to the more marginalized stories of this era, before and during the Cultural Revolution itself. One of the most moving, harrowing first-hand accounts recently made available of this period is *Blood Letters: The Untold Story of Lin Zhao, a Martyr in Mao's China* (ed. and trans. Lian Xi, London and New York: Basic Books, 2018). The title is derived from the fact that Lin's letters were written largely with her own blood when ink was taken away from her. In sometimes almost unbearably poignant detail they describe intimately the costs of dissent in the period of most intense Maoist fervour.

If we want to come to terms with contemporary China and the series of questions raised by its history, then we need to engage with a vast literature, one that grows even more vast with each passing month. A very personal selection of material produced in recent years which has helped the author of this book think through these issues a little bit more clearly would need to include Yasheng Huang's superb, and empirically rich, *Capitalism with Chinese Characteristics* (Cambridge: Cambridge University Press, 2008), which attempts to answer the question of what precisely socialism with market principles might be by taking cases studies like that of Shanghai and showing the extraordinary contradictions in the city's model. Yu Keping, a key contemporary thinker in the PRC, offers an attempt to show the possibilities of one-party political pluralism in *Democracy is a Good Thing: Essays on Politics, Society, and Culture in Contemporary China* (Washington, DC: Brookings

University Press, 2009). It has to be said that Yu's book comes from a time when the political atmosphere was a little more creative than it became in the years after Xi Jinping came to power.

Jinghan Zeng's *The Chinese Communist Party's Capacity to Rule: Ideology, Legitimacy and Party Cohesion* (Basingstoke: Palgrave Macmillan, 2016) is a good overview of the kind of entity the Party is and why it is unique. Frank N. Pieke in *Knowing China: A Twenty-First-Century Guide* (Cambridge: Cambridge University Press, 2016) successfully attempts the hard task of trying to explain China within its own terms. Jean-Pierre Cabestan's *China Tomorrow: Democracy or Dictatorship?* (Lanham, Md, and Boulder, Colo.: Rowman & Littlefield, 2019) bravely addresses a question once much more popular, about the future trajectory of reform in the country. *China's Future?* (Cambridge: Polity Press, 2016) by David Shambaugh is more convinced of the unsustainability of the current governance model practised by Beijing, and offers not one but several potential scenarios for where things could go. Xin Liu's *Moralization of China* (Singapore: World Scientific, 2018) is a sometimes frustrating but sporadically stimulating argument about the search for values in a country where its core belief system has often proved vulnerable and hard for outsiders to understand. Similar questions are addressed, though in a very different way, in *Deep China: The Moral Life of the Person* (Berkeley: University of California Press, 2011) by psychologist

Arthur Kleinman and a group of fellow researchers, and it is one of the most rewarding books produced on contemporary China so far.

Notes

Chapter 1 China's Arduous March to Modernity

1 Ge Zhaoguang, *What is China? Territory, Ethnicity, Culture, and History*, trans. Michael Gibbs Hill (Cambridge, Mass.: Belknap Press of Harvard University Press, 2018), 19.

2 Ibid., 21.

3 Xi Jinping, 'Address to the First Session of the 12th National People's Congress', 17 March 2013, in *The Governance of China*, Vol. 1 (Beijing: Foreign Languages Press, 2014), 41.

4 Timothy Brook, *Great State: China and the World* (London: Profile Books, 2019).

5 Chiang Kai-shek, *China's Destiny and Chinese Economic Theory* (New York: Roy Publishers, 1947), 41.

6 Mao Zedong, *Selected Works of Mao Tse-Tung*, Vol. 2 (Peking: Foreign Languages Press, 1966), 307.

7 Kenneth Pomeranz, *The Great Divergence: China, Europe, and the Making of the Modern World Economy* (Princeton and Oxford: Princeton University Press, 2000), 16.

8 J. L. Cranmer-Byng (ed.), *An Embassy to China: Being the Journal Kept by Lord Macartney During his Embassy to the Emperor Ch'ien-lung 1793–1794* (London: Longmans, 1962), 164.

9 Franz Schurmann and Orville Schell (eds), *China Readings 1: Imperial China* (Harmondsworth: Penguin, 1967), 284.

10 Ibid., 7.

11 Ibid., 7.

12 Chiang, *China's Destiny*, 43.

13 Ibid., 92.

14 Mao, *Selected Works*, Vol. 2, 309.

15 Ibid., 329.

16 See EdgarSnow, *China's Long Revolution* (London: Hutchinson, 1971).

17 Zheng Wang, *Never Forget National Humiliation: Historical Memory in Chinese Politics and Foreign Relations* (New York: Columbia University Press, 2012), 68–9.

Chapter 2 China Reconstructs (1949–1958)

1 A. John Jowett, 'Patterns of Literacy in the People's Republic of China', *GeoJournal* Vol. 18, No. 4 (June 1989), 417.

2 Chinese National Bureau of Statistics, 'Basic Statistics on National Population Census in 1953, 1964, 1982, 1990, 2000 and 2010', *http://www.stats.gov.cn/tjsj/Ndsj/2011/html/D0305e.htm*.

3 Barry Naughton, *The Chinese Economy: Transitions and Growth* (Cambridge, Mass.: MIT Press, 2006), 50.

4 Ibid., 51, 50.

5 Jeremy Brown and Paul G. Pickowicz, 'The Early Years of the People's Republic of China: An Introduction', in Brown and Pickowicz (eds), *Dilemmas of Victory: The Early Years of the People's Republic of China* (Cambridge, Mass.: Harvard University Press, 2007), 1.

6 Andrew Walder, *China Under Mao: A Revolution Derailed* (Cambridge, Mass.: Harvard University Press, 2015).

7 See Congressional Research Service, 'China's Economic Rise: History, Trends, Challenges, and Implications for the United States', updated 25 June 2019, 2, available at *https://fas.org/sgp/crs/row/RL33534.pdf*.

8 See data at *https://en.wikipedia.org/wiki/Historical_GDP_of_China*.

9 Marie-Claire Bergère, *Shanghai: China's Gateway to Modernity*, trans. Janet Lloyd (Stanford: Stanford University Press, 2009), 158.

10 Mao Zedong, *Selected Works of Mao Tse-tung*, Vol. 5 (Peking: Foreign Languages Press, 1977), 101.

11 Ibid., 402.

12 Roderick MacFarquhar, Timothy Cheek, and Eugene Wu (eds), *The Secret Speeches of Chairman Mao: From the Hundred*

Flowers to the Great Leap Forward (Cambridge, Mass.: Harvard University Press, 1989), 154.

13 A. Doak Barnett, *Cadres, Bureaucracy and Political Power in Communist China* (New York and London: Columbia University Press, 1967), 429.

14 See Mao Tse-tung, 'Report on the Investigation of the Peasant Movement in Hunan', in *Selected Works of Mao Tse-tung*, Vol. 1 (Peking: Foreign Languages Press, 1966), 23ff.

15 Mark Selden (ed.), *The People's Republic of China: A Documentary History of Revolutionary Change* (New York and London: Monthly Review Press, 1979), 240.

16 Ibid., 335.

17 Denis Twitchett and John K. Fairbank (eds), *The Cambridge History of China: Vol. 14: The People's Republic, Part 1: The Emergence of Revolutionary China 1949–1965* (Cambridge: Cambridge University Press, 1986), 87.

18 Robert J. Lifton, 'Peking's Thought Reform: Group Therapy to Save Your Soul', in Franz Schurmann and Orville Schell (eds), *China Readings 3: Communist China* (Harmondsworth: Penguin, 1968), 136.

19 Alexander V. Pantsov and Steven I. Levine, *Mao: The Real Story* (New York: Simon & Schuster, 2012), 457.

20 Yang Jiang, *Xizao* (Beijing: Sanlian Shudian Publishing, 1988). Also available in English as *Baptism*, trans. Judith M. Amory and Yaohua Shi (Hong Kong: Hong Kong University Press, 2007).

21 John W. Garver, *China's Quest: The History of the Foreign Relations of the People's Republic of China* (Oxford: Oxford University Press, 2016), 29.

Chapter 3 The Years of Dissent (1958–1966)

1 Stuart Schram (ed.), *Mao Tse-tung Unrehearsed: Talks and Letters 1956–71* (Harmondsworth: Penguin, 1974), 107.

2 Ibid., 146.

3 Ibid., 116.

4 MacFarquhar et al. (eds), *The Secret Speeches of Chairman Mao*, 235.

5 Ibid., 222.

6 W. J. Jenner (ed.), *Fragrant Weeds: Chinese Short Stories Once Labelled as 'Poisonous Weeds'*, trans. Geremie Barmé and Bennett Lee (Hong Kong: Joint Publishing Co., 1983), 22–3.

7 Mei Zhi, *F: Hu Feng's Prison Years*, ed. and trans. Gregor Benton (London: Verso, 2013), 23.

8 Selden (ed.), *The People's Republic of China*, 382.

9 Franz Schurmann, *Ideology and Organization in Communist China* (Berkeley: University of California Press, 1966), 74.

10 Naughton, *The Chinese Economy*, 69.

11 Central Committee of the Communist Party of China, 'Resolution on certain questions in the history of our party since the founding of the People's Republic of China', June 1981, available at *https://www.marxists.org/subject/china/docu ments/cpc/history/01.htm*.

12 The work by Jasper Becker, *Hungry Ghosts: Mao's Secret Famine* (New York: Free Press, 1996), was the earliest in English that focused on the famine, and for this reason had value. But Yang's work (see note 13) has far greater amounts of data and context.

13 Yang Jisheng, *Tombstone: The Untold Story of Mao's Great Famine*, trans. Stacy Mosher and Guo Jian (London and New York: Allen Lane, 2012), 13.

14 Schram (ed.), *Mao Tse-tung Unrehearsed*, 194.

15 Ralph A. Thaxton, Jr, *Catastrophe and Contention in Rural China: Mao's Great Leap Forward Famine and the Origins of Righteous Resistance in Da Fo Village* (Cambridge: Cambridge University Press, 2008), 326.

16 Selden (ed.), *The People's Republic of China*, 508.

17 'Statement by Peking on Nuclear Test' issued by Xinhua, 17 October 1964, in *New York Times*, available at *https://www. nytimes.com/1964/10/17/archives/statement-by-peking-on-nucl ear-test.html*.

18 Zhou Enlai, *Selected Works*, Vol. 2 (Beijing: Foreign Languages Press, 1984), 460–1.

19 Alexander V. Pantsov and Steven I. Levine, *Deng Xiaoping: A Revolutionary Life* (Oxford: Oxford University Press, 2015), 217.

20 Ibid., 221.
21 See Roderick MacFarquhar, *The Origins of the Cultural Revolution*, Vol. 3 (Oxford: Oxford University Press, 1997).

Chapter 4 The Great Proletariat Cultural Revolution (1966–1976)

1 CPC Central Committee, 'Decisions Concerning the Great Proletariat Cultural Revolution', *Peking Review*, No. 33, 1966, 6.
2 Quoted in David Milton, Nancy Milton, and Franz Schurmann (eds), *The China Reader 4: People's China* (New York: Random House, 1974), 253.
3 Li Zhensheng, *Red-Color News Soldier* (London: Phaidon, 2003), 105. 'Black gang element' was a term of abuse in Chinese referring to people who were from bad, disloyal backgrounds.
4 'Stinking number nines' was a term of abuse for intellectuals, referring to their rank in the social hierarchy of nine classes of people promoted by the Maoist Communists.
5 Quoted in Milton et al. (eds), *The China Reader 4*, 239.
6 Ibid., 248–9.
7 Ibid., 279.
8 See Roderick MacFarquhar and Michael Schoenhals, *Mao's Last Revolution* (Cambridge, Mass.: Belknap Press of Harvard University Press, 2006), 33. For the membership of the group over 1966 into 1968, see Andrew G. Walder, *Fractured Rebellion: The Beijing Red Guard Movement* (Cambridge, Mass.: Harvard University Press, 2009), 18–19.
9 Walder, *Fractured Rebellion*, 3.
10 Quoted in Michael Schoenhals (ed.), *China's Cultural Revolution 1966–1969: Not a Dinner Party* (Armonk, NY, and London: M. E. Sharpe, 1996), 149.
11 Chi Hsin, *Teng Hsiao-ping: A Political Biography* (Hong Kong: Cosmos Books, 1978), 64.
12 Yao Wenyuan, 'On the New Historical Play, "Dismissal of Hai Rui"', November 1965, available at *https://www.marxists.org/archive/yao-wenyuan/1965/november/10.htm*.

13 Schram (ed.), *Mao Tse-tung Unrehearsed*, 254.

14 Ibid., 258.

15 Schoenhals (ed.), *China's Cultural Revolution 1966–1969*, 198.

16 Ibid., 201.

17 Ibid., 214–17.

18 Mark O'Neill, *The Miraculous History of China's Two Palace Museums* (Hong Kong: Joint Publishing, 2015), 263.

19 See Sheila Melvin and Jindong Cai, *Beethoven in China* (London: Penguin, 2015), 82–3.

20 Zheng Yi, *Scarlet Memorial: Tales of Cannibalism in Modern China*, ed. and trans. T. P. Sym (Boulder, Colo.: Westview Press, 1996), 90.

21 Yang Su, *Collective Killings in Rural China During the Cultural Revolution* (Cambridge: Cambridge University Press, 2011), chapter 8.

22 Tan Hecheng, *The Killing Wind: A Chinese County's Descent into Madness During the Cultural Revolution*, trans. Stacey Mosher and Guo Jian (Oxford: Oxford University Press, 2017), 159.

23 Yan Jiaqi and Gao Yuan, *Wenhua da Geming: Shi Nian Shi*, Vol. 1 (Taipei: Lianzhi Publishing, 1990), 160–2.

24 Ba Jin, *Random Thoughts*, trans. Geremie Barmé (Hong Kong: Joint Publishing, 1984), 76.

25 MacFarquhar and Schoenhals, *Mao's Last Revolution*, 293.

26 Yao Ming-le, *The Conspiracy and Murder of Mao's Heir* (London: Collins, 1983), 30. According to Jen Qiu's study, Lin probably suffered from fragile physical and mental health, showing symptoms of neurasthaenia and hypochondria. He may even have had manic depression, which perhaps explains some of his curious behaviour, such as inhaling fumes from a revved motorcycle and claiming these were beneficial for one's health! See Jen Qiu, *The Culture of Power: The Lin Biao Incident in the Cultural Revolution* (Stanford: Stanford University Press, 1999), 145–6.

27 Milton et al. (eds), *The China Reader 4*, 286.

28 MacFarquhar and Schoenhals, *Mao's Last Revolution*, 291.

29 Ibid., 292.

30 Goran Leijonhufvud, *Going Against the Tide: On Dissent and*

Big Character Posters in China (London: Curzon Press, 1990), 125.

31 Ibid.

32 Ezra Vogel, *Deng Xiaoping and the Transformation of China* (Cambridge, Mass.: Belknap Press of Harvard University Press, 2011), 56–7.

33 John King Fairbank, *The Great Chinese Revolution: 1800–1985* (London: Chatto & Windus, 1987), 341.

Chapter 5 Reform and Opening Up (1976–1989)

1 The quote, relayed via Premier Wen Jiabao in 2004 during a speech he made, is cited in Willy Wo-Wap Lam's *Chinese Politics in the Hu Jintao Era: New Leaders, New Challenges* (Armonk, NY, and London: M. E. Sharpe, 2006), 109. It does not, however, exist in Deng's *Collected Speeches*, though it may have been one of a number of extempore remarks that Deng made during this tour.

2 Selden (ed.), *The People's Republic of China*, 654.

3 Ibid., 659.

4 Roger Irvine, *Forecasting China's Future: Dominance or Collapse?* (London: Routledge, 2016), 22.

5 Ibid., 22.

6 Frederick C. Teiwes and Warren Sun, 'China's New Economic Policy Under Hua Guofeng: Party Consensus and Party Myths', *China Journal*, No. 66, July 2011, 2.

7 Orville Schell and David Shambaugh (eds), *The China Reader: The Reform Era* (New York: Vintage Books, 1999), 24.

8 Ibid., 27.

9 Ibid., 29.

10 Wei Jingsheng, *The Courage to Stand Alone: Letters from Prison and Other Writings*, trans. Kristina M. Torgeson (New York: Viking, 1997), 234.

11 Ibid., 238.

12 Ibid., 209.

13 See Jonathan Spence, *The Gate of Heavenly Peace: The Chinese and Their Revolution, 1895–1980* (Harmondsworth: Penguin, 1982), 408–15.

14   Schell and Shambaugh (eds), *The China Reader: The Reform Era*, 47.

15   Yasheng Huang, *Capitalism with Chinese Characteristics: Entrepreneurship and the State* (Cambridge: Cambridge University Press, 2008), 52.

16   Ibid., 53.

17   Ibid., 56.

18   Jao Ho Chung, *Centrifugal Empire: Central Local Relations in China* (New York: Columbia University Press, 2016), 21.

19   See the work of Peter Nolan on this, in particular *China and the Global Economy: National Champions, Industrial Policy and the Big Business Revolution* (London: Palgrave Macmillan, 2001).

20   Chung, *Centrifugal Empire*, 27.

21   Quoted in Yasheng Huang, *Selling China* (Cambridge: Cambridge University Press, 2003), 308.

22   Victor Nee and Sonja Opper, *Capitalism from Below: Markets and Institutional Change in China* (Cambridge, Mass.: Harvard University Press, 2012), 38.

23   This is meticulously documented in Frederic C. Teiwes and Warren Sun, *Paradoxes of Post-Mao Rural Reform: Initial Steps Towards a New Chinese Countryside, 1976–1981* (London and New York: Routledge, 2016).

24   Source: *http://worldpopulationreview.com/world-cities/shenzhen-population/*.

25   Gov.cn, 'Premier Calls for Further Reform, Ideological Emancipation', 21 August 2010, *www.china.org.cn/china/2010-08/22/content_20763900.htm.*

26   Guardian Datablog: 'China GDP: How It Has Changed since 1980', *https://www.theguardian.com/news/datablog/2012/mar/23/china-gdp-since-1980*.

27   George J. Church, 'China: Old Wounds: Deng Xiaoping', *Time*, 6 January 1986, *http://content.time.com/time/subscriber/article/0,33009,1074879-9,00.html*.

28   Quoted in Geremie Barmé and John Minford, *Seeds of Fire: Chinese Voices of Conscience* (Newcastle upon Tyne: Bloodaxe Books, 1989), 345.

29 Mark Elvin, *Changing Stories in the Chinese World* (Stanford: Stanford University Press, 1997), 177.
30 Ben Hillman, *Patronage and Power: Local State Networks and Party-State Resilience in Rural China* (Stanford: Stanford University Press, 2014), 138.
31 Schell and Shambaugh (eds), *The China Reader: The Reform Era*, 54.
32 Ibid., 96.
33 Lam, *Chinese Politics in the Hu Jintao Era*, 8.
34 Andrew J. Nathan and Perry Link (eds), *The Tiananmen Papers* (London: Little, Brown and Company, 2001), 202.
35 Ibid., 358.
36 Ibid., 359.
37 See Timothy Brook, *Quelling the People: The Military Suppression of the Beijing Democracy Movement* (Stanford: Stanford University Press, 1998), 151–69.

Chapter 6 Starting Over after Tiananmen (1989–2001)

1 Recordings of him managed to be compiled, in his old age, into a book documenting his side of the story of the lead-up to June 1989. See Zhao Ziyang, *Prisoner of the State*, trans. Bao Pu (New York: Simon & Schuster, 2009).
2 Nathan and Link (eds), *The Tiananmen Papers*, 408.
3 Ibid., 409.
4 Schell and Shambaugh (eds), *The China Reader: The Reform Era*, 208.
5 Robert S. Ross, *Chinese Security Policy: Structure, Power and Politics* (London and New York: Routledge, 2009), 245.
6 Deng Xiaoping, 'Excerpts from Talks Given in Wuchang, Shenzhen, Zhuhai and Shanghai', January to February 1992, available at *https://dengxiaopingworks.wordpress.com/2013/03/18/excerpts-from-talks-given-in-wuchang-shenzhen-zhuhai-and-shanghai/*.
7 Ibid.
8 David Shambaugh, *China's Communist Party: Atrophy and Adaptation* (Berkeley: University of California Press, 2008), 64.

9   Ibid., 59.

10 Pai Hsien-yung, *Taipei People* (Hong Kong: Chinese University Press, 2000), 2.

11 Quoted in Edward Friedman, 'China's Changing Taiwan Policy', *American Journal of Chinese Studies*, Vol. 14, No. 2, October 2007, 123.

12 See 'Deng's Heirs Ignore His Advice – China Spat with Japan', *Economist*, 23 September 2010, at *https://www.economist.com/asia/2010/09/23/dengs-heirs-ignore-his-advice*.

13 Schell and Shambaugh (eds), *The China Reader: The Reform Era*, 498.

14 Deng Xiaoping, *Fundamental Issues in Present-Day China* (Beijing: Foreign Languages Press, 1987), 48–51.

15 Full text of Sino-British Joint Declaration, 1984, available at *https://www.cmab.gov.hk/en/issues/jd2.htm*.

16 Schell and Shambaugh (eds), *The China Reader: The Reform Era*, 127.

17 Naughton, *The Chinese Economy*, 218.

18 Anita Chan, *China's Workers Under Assault: The Exploitation of Labour in a Globalizing Economy* (Armonk, NY, and London: M. E. Sharpe, 2001), 10.

19 From Human Rights Watch, 'China: Nipped in the Bud: The Suppression of the China Democracy Movement', 1 September 2000, at *https://www.hrw.org/report/2000/09/01/china-nipped-bud/suppression-china-democracy-party*.

20 Human Rights Watch detailed some of these in 2002: *https://www.hrw.org/reports/2002/china02/china0802-11.htm*.

21 Schell and Shambaugh (eds), *The China Reader: The Reform Era*, 123.

22 Ibid., 124.

23 Bruce J. Dickson, *Red Capitalists in China: The Party, Private Entrepreneurs, and Prospects for Political Change* (Cambridge: Cambridge University Press, 2003), 22.

24 Yasheng Huang, *Selling China: Foreign Direct Investment During the Reform Era* (Cambridge: Cambridge University Press, 2003), 122–3.

25 China.org.cn, 'What is "Three Represents" CPC Theory?', *www.china.org.cn/english/zhuanti/3represents/68735.htm*.

Chapter 7 The Hu Jintao Era (2001–2012)

1 Cheng Li, *China's Leaders: The New Generation* (Lanham, Md, and Boulder, Colo.: Rowman & Littlefield Publishers, 2001), 44.
2 Data from *https://www.theguardian.com/news/datablog/2012/mar/23/china-gdp-since-1980*.
3 Joe Studwell, *The China Dream: The Quest for the Last Great Untapped Market on Earth* (London: Profile, 2002).
4 Statista, 'Car Parc in China from 2009 to 2019', *https://www.statista.com/statistics/285306/number-of-car-owners-in-china/*.
5 China Marketing, 'Chinese Outbound Tourists', *https://www.marketingtochina.com/strategic-report-for-global-hospitality-ceos-wanted-target-china/*.
6 Chan Koonchang, *The Fat Years*, trans. Michael S. Duke (London: Random House, 2011), 38–9.
7 Cao Jinqing, *China Along the Yellow River: Reflections on Rural Society* (New York: RoutledgeCurzon, 2005).
8 Chen Guidi and Wu Chuntao, *Will the Boat Sink the Water? The Life of China's Peasants* (London: Public Affairs, 2006), 151.
9 Bruce J. Dickson, *The Dictator's Dilemma: The Chinese Communist Party's Strategy for Survival* (Oxford: Oxford University Press, 2016), 142.
10 Quoted in Kerry Brown, *Ballot Box China: Grassroots Democracy in the Final Major One-Party State* (London: Zed Books, 2011), 33.
11 Niall MacCarthy, 'China Now Boasts More Than 800 Million Internet Users and 98% of Them Are Mobile' (infographic), Forbes, 23 August 2018, *https://www.forbes.com/sites/niallmccarthy/2018/08/23/china-now-boasts-more-than-800-million-internet-users-and-98-of-them-are-mobile-infographic/#421d4b197092*.
12 Arthur Kleinman, Yunxiang Yan, Jing Jun, Sing Lee, Everatt Zhang, Pan Tianshu, Wu Fei, and Guo Jinhua, *Deep China: The Moral Life of the Person* (Berkeley: University of California Press, 2011), 60.
13 Ibid., 30.

14 OECD, 'Economic Survey of China', 2005, available at *https:// www.oecd.org/china/economicsurveyofchina2005executivesumm ary.htm*.

15 Jie Chen and Bruce J. Dickson, *Allies of the State: China's Private Entrepreneurs and Democratic Change* (Cambridge, Mass.: Harvard University Press, 2010), 37.

16 Zhou Tianyong, Wang Changjiang, and Wang Anling (eds), *Gong Jian: Zhongguo Zhengzhi Tizhi Gaige Yanjiu Baogao, Shi Qi da Yihou* (Urumqi: Xinjiang Production Cors Publication House, 2007).

17 Gloria Davies, *Worrying About China: The Language of Chinese Critical Inquiry* (Cambridge, Mass.: Harvard University Press, 2007), 1.

18 Liu Xiaobo, *No Enemies, No Hatred*, eds Perry Link, Tienchi Martin-Liao, and Liu Xia (Cambridge, Mass.: Belknap Press of Harvard University Press), 74.

Chapter 8 China's Dream Realized under Xi Jinping?

1 Michael Martina and Benjamin Kang Lim, 27 October 2016, 'China Xi Anointed "Core Leader" on Par with Mao, Deng', Reuters, *https://uk.reuters.com/article/uk-china-politics/chinas-xi-anointed-core-leader-on-par-with-mao-deng-idUKKCN12R 1QW*.

2 See Jane Perlez, 'Q and A: Geremie R. Barmé: On Understanding Xi Jinping', *New York Times*, 8 November 2015, *https://sinosphere.blogs.nytimes.com/2015/11/08/china-xi-jinping-geremie-barme-maoing-xi-jinping/*.

3 Xu Zhangrun, 'Imminent Fears, Immediate Hopes – Beijing Jeremiad', trans. Geremie R. Barmé, *China Heritage*, 1 August 2018, *http://chinaheritage.net/journal/imminent-fears-immediate-hopes-a-beijing-jeremiad/*.

4 Xi Jinping, 'The People's Wish for a Good Life is Our Goal', 15 November 2012, in *The Governance of China*, Vol. 1 (Beijing: Foreign Languages Press, 2014), 3.

5 Ibid., 29.

6 Ibid., 37.

7 Ibid., 38.

8 Andrew Wedeman, *Double Paradox: Rapid Growth and Rising Corruption in China* (Ithaca, NY, and London: Cornell University Press, 2012), 4.

9 See Konstantinos Tsimonis, 'Sharpening "Swords" and Strengthening "Cages": Anticorruption under Xi,' in Kerry Brown (ed.), *China's 19th Party Congress: Start of a New Era* (Singapore: World Scientific, 2018), 57.

10 Ross, *Chinese Security Policy*, 59.

11 Yan Xuetong, *Ancient Chinese Thought, Modern Chinese Power*, trans. Edmund Ryden (Princeton and Oxford: Princeton University Press, 2011), 99.

12 Ibid., 179.

13 Ibid., 153.

Index